Jacob of Sarug's Homilies on Jacob

Texts from Christian Late Antiquity

58

Series Editor

George Anton Kiraz

TeCLA (Texts from Christian Late Antiquity) is a series presenting ancient Christian texts both in their original languages and with accompanying contemporary English translations.

Jacob of Sarug's Homilies on Jacob

On Jacob's Revelation at Bethel
and
On our Lord and Jacob, on the Church and Rachel and on Leah and the Synagogue

Translated by

Dana Miller

Edited with Notes and Introduction by

Mary T. Hansbury

2020

Gorgias Press LLC, 954 River Road, Piscataway, NJ, 08854, USA

www.gorgiaspress.com

Copyright © 2020 by Gorgias Press LLC

All rights reserved under International and Pan-American Copyright Conventions. No part of this publication may be reproduced, stored in a retrieval system or transmitted in any form or by any means, electronic, mechanical, photocopying, recording, scanning or otherwise without the prior written permission of Gorgias Press LLC.

2020

ISBN 978-1-4632-4189-6   **ISSN 1935-6846**

```
Library of Congress Cataloging-in-Publication
Data

A Cataloging-in-Publication Record is available
from the Library of Congress.
```

Printed in the United States of America

TABLE OF CONTENTS

Table of Contents v
Abbreviations vii
Introduction 1
   Outline 1
   Eye of Prophecy 4
   Other Parallels in the Writings of Jacob 6
   Jacob in an Exegetical Tradition 6
   Summary 9
      On the Vision of Jacob at Bethel [#74] 9
      On the Church and Rachel [#75] 11
Text and Translation 13
Homily 74: A Homily on Jacob's Revelation at Bethel 14
   I. Love as a Principle of Exegesis 14
   II. Divine Revelations 18
      1. The Staff and the Cross 18
      2. The Ladder and the Cross 20
   III. Jacob's Responses 34
      1. Request of Blessings 34
      2. Placing of the First Stone of the Church 36
      3. Vows of Poverty and Renunciation 44
      4. Jacob invokes the Our Father 46
Homily 75: A Homily On Our Lord and Jacob, On the Church and Rachel, and On Leah and the Synagogue 54
Bibliography of Works Cited 87
Index 93
   Biblical References 93
   Index of Key Terms 93

ABBREVIATIONS

CSCO	Corpus Scriptorum Christianorum Orientalium (Louvain).
ETL	Ephemerides Theologicae Lovanienses (Leuven).
Harp	The Harp: a Review of Syriac and Oriental Studies (Kottayam).
JCSSS	Journal of the Canadian Society for Syriac Studies.
JEasternCS	Journal of Eastern Christian Studies (Leuven).
JSS	Journal of Semitic Studies (Manchester/Oxford).
LM	Le Muséon (Louvain la Neuve).
NAKG	Nadirlandsch Archief voor Kerkgeschiedenis.
OCA	Orientalia Christiana Analecta (Rome).
OCP	Orientalia Christiana Periodica (Rome).
OS	L'Orient Syrien (Vernon).
PdO	Parole de l'Orient (Kaslik, Lebanon).
PO	Patrologia Orientalis (Turnhout).
RTP	Revue de Théologie et de Philosophie (Louvain/Lausanne).
SEERI	St. Ephrem Ecumenical Research Institute (Kottayam).
Sob/ECR	Sobornost incorporating Eastern Churches Review (Oxford).

SS	Scriptores Syri (in CSCO).
StPatr	Studia Patristica (Kalamazoo/Leuven/Berlin/Oxford).
SVTQ	Saint Vladimir's Theological Quarterly (New York).
TeCLA	Texts from Christian Late Antiquity (Gorgias Press).
TS	Theological Studies (Baltimore).

INTRODUCTION

> INFORMATION ON THESE HOMILIES
> Homily Title: Jacob's Revelation at Bethel
> Source of Text: *Homiliae Selectae Mar-Jacob Sarugensis*, edited by Paul Bedjan (Paris-Leipzig: Harrassowitz, 1907), 2nd ed. Piscataway: Gorgias Press, 2006), vol. 3, pp. 192–207. [Homily 74]
>
> Homily Title: [Homily 75] On our Lord and Jacob, On the Church and Rachel and on Leah and the Synagogue
> Source of Text: *Homiliae Selectae Mar-Jacob Sarugensis,* edited by Paul Bedjan (Paris-Leipzig: Harrassowitz, 1907), 2nd ed. Piscataway: Gorgias Press, 2006), vol. 3, pp. 208–223. [Homily 75]

OUTLINE

Jacob emphasizes love in relation to Scripture. Faith as indicated by Ephrem is never neglected. But there is in Jacob's *Letters* and *mimre* an insistence on the power of love as an exegetical principle. It does not seem formulaic or even only an aspect of cognition. Rather, it is intrinsic to his soteriology which underlies his understanding of Scripture. According to Boulos Sony, the Christological controversies of his time pushed Jacob deeper into Scripture, where instead of definitions, he found the mystery (*râzâ*) of Christ on every page.[1] According to Jacob: "The Scriptures provide the God-experience of the people of God in various forms of human communication. Rather than providing divine truths they furnish

---

[1] See Boulos Sony, "La Methode Exegétique de Jacques de Saroug," 83–85.

experiences of divine-human encounter."[2] Thus Scripture is an ongoing revelation, through its mysteries, of God's love for mankind and the only adequate and effective response according to Jacob is love.[3]

Thus Jacob begins this homily:

> Love alone possesses an ear that tries every word
> and it grows not weary whenever it inclines to listen.
> For it was also through love that they drew near to God.
> One must attend to the histories of the righteous with love,
> for it was through love that they drew near to God.

Prayer and love for the word of God and faith are the basic requisites for the understanding of the Scriptures. This exegetical activity is a science, like a lamp, that helps one to enter into the Scriptures. According to Jacob of Serug the same spirit works through the inspired writers of the Scriptures, the interpreters, and the readers or hearers of the Scriptures. Rather than providing defined truths they furnish an experience of divine-human encounters. The aim of exegetical activity, according to Jacob, is to bring out the concealed mystery (*râzâ*) into the light.

Some have misunderstood Jacob of Serug's symbolic thinking such as R. Chesnut who tends to mistakenly see it as Gnostic.[4] This set back the understanding of Mar Jacob until recently.[5]

In the second section, *Divine Revelations*, Mar Jacob sees in the biblical account a foreshadowing of both the Cross of Christ and His death. The angels, "they beheld him how he embraced his staff and fell asleep upon the mountain peak, and their assemblies encompassed him to gaze upon the image of the Crucifixion."[6] Jacob's slumber depicts the mystery of the death of the Son of God. And his staff is a symbol of the Cross. He took the staff with him when he went on the journey that it might represent the Son's

---

[2] T. Kollamparampil, *Select Festal Homilies*, 26.

[3] See Hansbury, "Love as an Exegetical Principle."

[4] See R. Chesnut, *Three Monophysite Christologies*.

[5] See Kollamparampil, *Salvation in Christ*, 20–21 and see A. Golitzin, "The Image and Glory of God in Jacob of Serug's Homily," 323–30.

[6] See lines trans. 61–62; cf. Gen 28.12 (Hom.#74).

Cross. Not only does Jacob's sleep depict the scene of the Crucifixion, but it prefigures the betrothal of Christ to His Church.[7]

In the third section, *Jacob Responds*, it becomes evident how God's providence guided Jacob to that place where he slept that he might be the one who betroths the Church to the Son of God. Mar Jacob says that the stone Jacob uses as a pillow is a symbol of the Church. "She will return not as a symbol but as the community professing its faith in the divinity of Christ. The rock is an image of the house of the King's bride and her bridal chamber where the mystery will be celebrated."[8]

> Bring oil and pour it over the stone, which is the Church,
> and represent it for Me, for after a time it shall be restored!
> Lay a foundation for the great house of the King's Bride,
> where all the righteous will establish all their offspring!
> Prepare for Me the bridal chamber, so that the mystery might enter and be celebrated there,
> until I Myself make the great wedding feast through the entire world![9]

This quote leaves no doubt to the fact that, in the mind of Mar Jacob, the stone used by the Patriarch as a pillow refers to the Church. The stone is just a foreshadowing of what is to come. The Church shall no longer be depicted by symbols, for she will return.[10] The son of Isaac did not build the entire structure of the Church but laid down its cornerstone. The righteous who come after him will continue building upon it until the Son of God reveals the whole structure.

---

[7] See Elkhoury, *Types and Symbols*, 270–73.

[8] Idem, p. 273.

[9] Trans. lines 243–48 (Hom. #74).

[10] See Elkhoury, *Types and Symbols*, 76. And see his ch. 2: The Church, Building on Golgotha.

EYE OF PROPHECY[11]

'Prophecy is the solution that God chose to solve the problem'. His prophets maintain his unicity and depict his hidden Son through prophecies. The prophecies make known the Only-Begotten through types and symbols. These types and symbols contain the whole truth about the Son and are recorded in the Old Testament. "This means that God manifested his Beloved through the O.T. But he had covered it as if with a veil to camouflage the coming of his Son."[12]

Elkhoury quotes from the Veil of Moses:

> This is what the veil on Moses' face symbolizes;
> that the words of prophecy are veiled;
> the Lord covered Moses' face for this reason,
> that it might be a type for prophecy, which is also veiled.
> The Father kept the Son in concealment, without anyone being aware, but He wished to reveal this matter to the world in symbolic terms; He wished to speak about His Beloved One through prophecy
> and so covered up Moses to make him a figure for prophecy
> so that, whenever a prophet arose on earth to speak, it might be recognized that his words were veiled from those who heard them,
> that there was something hidden, concealed in the matter of which he spoke, and for his words to be understood, it requires an awareness of what they symbolize.
> Thus He cried out in the prophet, 'I have a secret, I have a secret'.
> So that the world might be aware that the prophecy contained mysteries: the words and the actions of prophecy are veiled;
> it hides its contents in parables so that they might not be recognized;
> it devises figures and utters its words as if in secret

---

[11] See Elkhoury, "Jesus Christ, the Eye of Prophecy," a fine article which concentrates on prophecy.

[12] Elkhoury, "Eye of Prophecy," 3.

so that the world might not become openly aware of the Son of God.[13]

For Mar Jacob, the Book of the Father, i.e. the Old Testament, is a map illustrating the way of the Only-Begotten. The Book of the Father is filled with the types of the Son. There is not even one line in the O.T. that does not proclaim the way of the Son.[14]

The homily concludes (lines 290–336) with Jacob "tracing out the Church and making her steadfast through his prayers." (l. 276) And he invokes the Our Father. It is revealed to him. "Therefore let the world learn from me that what even I knew not." (l. 270) Jacob is dealing with an incident in the O.T. But for Mar Jacob this is not surprising as he believed that every word of the O.T. points to Christ.[15] Therefore Jacob asked only for clothing and bread so as to be a witness (Gen 28.20): "that in him the perfect path of apostleship might be depicted." (l. 282) He began to repeat the prayer commanded to the Lord's apostles so that they should never seek for more than for their daily bread. Therefore, for this reason, Jacob asked only for clothing and bread, so as to be a witness to the new doctrine of our Lord, revealed already in the O.T., according to Mar Jacob. He stresses that Jacob received the Lord's Prayer during the vision on the mountain. Before the Lord had sent the vision to Jacob, he had not known the prayer. However, after the vision, Jacob continues to anticipate what the apostles would later do. (l. 310–335)

---

[13] S. Brock, *Jacob of Serugh on the Veil of Moses*, lines 21–38.

[14] Elkhoury, "Jesus Christ, the Eye of Prophecy," 6.

[15] See F. Siroli, "Jacob of Serugh and the Lord's Prayer," pp. 27–34. She shows how the Lord's Prayer appears elsewhere as a revelation in homilies of Jacob: *On the Reception of the Holy Mysteries; The Kingdom of Heaven as Leaven; On Love.*

OTHER PARALLELS IN THE WRITINGS OF JACOB

As noted by Lange[16] the ladder spoken of in this homily is mentioned in other homilies of Mar Jacob. In his *Homélie sur la Nativité*,[17] it is the Son and not God the Father who revealed himself on the ladder. As if Mar Jacob saw Jacob's vision at Bethel as the Son's acting towards humanity and identifies the Lord of Gen. 28:13 with the Son.

The ladder of Bethel also appeared at the Lord's tomb in the *Homily on the Sunday of the Resurrection*.[18] "An awesome clamour of angels was heard from the air, a ladder of light was placed between the tomb and heaven, the one that had been seen by Jacob at Bethel; and the Lord was standing, not above it ready to descend, but below it, ready to ascend." The ladder combines the Lord's tomb with heaven.

Another image is that of Jacob acting as priest in the *Homélie contre les Juifs I*,[19] by anointing the foundation stone of God's sanctuary with sacred oil prefiguring Christ's activity and becoming an anticipation of the High Priest.

There is also the presence of the angels/Watchers together with the ladder(as in the Jacob at Bethel homily, l. 56–102) in *Drei Gedichte über den Apostel Thomas in Indien*.[20] The angels guard Thomas as they had surrounded Jacob at Bethel.

JACOB IN AN EXEGETICAL TRADITION

Both Aphrahat and Ephrem interpret Gen 28:10–22 in a typological way as does Mar Jacob.[21] Ephrem deals with Jacob's vision at

---

[16] See his very helpful article: "The Mystery of the Son Did Not Journey Without the Church". To be consulted for other insights as well concerning this homily (#74).

[17] Cf. F. Rilliet, *Six Homélies Festales en Prose*, l. 20, p. 32.

[18] Kollamparampil, *Select Festal Homilies*, "Sunday of the Resurrection," par. 10, p. 322.

[19] Cf. M. Albert: *Jacques de Saroug. Homélies contre les Juifs*, p. 57.

[20] See Strothmann, 296.

[21] For the reference to Aphrahat, see Lange, "Mystery of the Son," 216.

Bethel in his *Commentary on Genesis*, chapter 26.26.[22] Jacob and Ephrem agree that the angels use the ladder to ascend to heaven or to descend to earth. For both Jacob and Ephrem the oil is a symbol of Christ; and for both of them the stone over which Jacob pours out the oil of anointment stands symbolically for the Church. Other parallels may be seen in Ephrem's Hymns of Virginity[23] and in the Nisibene Hymns.[24] In the Commentary on the Diatessaron, the stone that Jacob placed under his head (Gen. 28.18) is identified with the stone at the tomb (Mt. 28.2) and its removal from the tomb "introduced the gentiles into the Church."[25]

To go beyond the confines of this homily, since it narrates only the beginning of the journey of the Church, it is helpful to consult the research of S.K. Joshua, *Church as Bride of Christ*. He delineates how Mar Jacob has the conviction that the betrothal between Christ and the Church was hidden in the prophecies.[26] Mt Sinai prefigures Christ's betrothal of the Church at Golgotha. Betrothal at the Jordan follows Sinai. Finally there is the Betrothal at Golgotha. For Mar Jacob, Jesus liberated the betrothed, the Church, from sin through these stages.[27]

This brings in research done by Murray and Brock which goes beyond the vision at Bethel but is part of the journey of the Church.[28]

And to conclude with the insightful article of Susan Harvey.[29] In the discussion of the Church's journey after the Incarnation the

---

[22] See Mathews and J.P. Amar (tr.) *St. Ephrem the Syrian. Selected Prose Works*, 173–74.

[23] See K. McVey (tr.) "Hymns on Virginity" #5, paragraph 15–16 in *Ephrem the Syrian, Hymns*.

[24] See the Nisibene Hymns no. 36, section 7 in S. Brock (tr.) *The Harp of the Spirit*.

[25] See Carmel McCarthy, *St Ephrem's Commentary on Tatian's Diatessaron*, XXI, 21.

[26] See also Bou Mansour, *Théologie de Jacques de Saroug* Vol 1, 147–160.

[27] See S.K. Joshua, *Church as the Bride of Christ*.

[28] See S. Brock, "Baptismal Themes in the Writings of Jacob of Sarug," 325–47. And see R. Murray "The Lance which Reopened Paradise: a Mysterious Reading in the Early Syriac Fathers."

perspective is less prophetic. But even here Mar Jacob uses images of the Church which open up its reality. S. Harvey writes about biblical women as images of Church in Jacob of Serug. In her article, Harvey considers three biblical women in particular: Jephthah's Daughter as the Bride of Blood (Judges 11);[30] Tamar, the daughter-in-law of Judah in a homily devoted to her story (Genesis 38);[31] the Sinful Woman, for which Jacob's homily combines the four Gospel accounts (Mt 26.6–13; Mk 14.3–9; Lk 7.36–50; Jn 12.1–11.[32]

Jephthah's Daughter is the only biblical character according to Mar Jacob who truly portrayed the image of Christ. In the Peshitta text of Judges 11 she is called *îḥîdâyûtâ*. Mar Jacob establishes her as 'the perfect Christological type' sacrificed by her father.[33] The implications of this typology will bear not only on Jephthah and his Daughter, but further on how to understand God's own self in the event of Jesus' crucifixion. So she is a revelation of the path of the Church.

Tamar is another symbol of Christ revealed along the road (*'urḥâ*) of salvation history. Mar Jacob calls her Bride of Light "Traveling down all the generations...so that God himself might be mingled (*ḥlṭ*) amongst humanity" (lines 49–51, Brock p. 294). Mar Jacob presents Tamar as the image of the Church betrothed to Christ, her heavenly Bridegroom, "because of the Mystery that was performed in her."[34]

Finally, the Sinful Woman like Tamar was driven by intense desire: her encounter with Christ, almost like a liturgy. The fragrance of her ointment mingled with her love, to become as incense – she was transformed into sacrifice and sacrificed, another image of Christ. Mar Jacob presents all three – Jephthah's Daughter, Tamar, the Sinful Woman – as images of the Church.

---

[29] S. Harvey "Bride of Blood, Bride of Light: Biblical Women as Images of Church in Jacob of Serug," 177–204.

[30] S. Harvey and Ophir Münz-Manor, *Jacob of Serug's Homily on Jephthah's Daughter*.

[31] S. Brock, "Jacob of Serug's verse homily on Tamar."

[32] S. Johnson, "The Sinful Woman: a memra by Jacob of Serug."

[33] See Harvey, "Bride of Blood", 187.

[34] Trans. Brock, lines 137–56.

In the 2nd homily (#75 On Our Lord and Jacob, On the Church and Rachel, and on Leah and the Synagogue) Jacob of Serug sees the patriarch Jacob as a type of Christ and the two sisters, Leah and Rachel, as types of the Synagogue and the Church respectively. From this he understood Jacob's betrothal and eventual marriage to the daughters of his mother's brother, Laban, as an image of Christ's betrothal to both the Synagogue and the Church.

Jacob of Serug dedicates a homily to the Synagogue and the Church.[35] Divided in six discussions: 1. The Synagogue lists the actions of God in its favor, particularly Exodus. Whereas the Church remembers God's mercy while it was corrupted by paganism. 2. The Synagogue calls out to Old Testament figures who with God authored its glorious past/history and will not abandon it. But the Church shows how the spiritual reading of Scripture is able to make visible the announcement of Christ, through the life and words of all the people. They can only reproach the blindness of Israel. 3. God promised the chosen People His alliance and the land of Canaan. Whereas the Church aspires to the heritage of the kingdom of God which is not of this world.[36] At the conclusion of these categories, Jacob adds 32 verses inspired by the Canticle of Canticles. All of this enriches the understanding of Synagogue and Church also in the context of "On the Church and Rachel and on Leah and the Synagogue."[37]

Summary

On the Vision of Jacob at Bethel [#74]

1. Introduction: 1–32

Power of love: 1–8.

---

[35] See M. Albert (tr.), "Mimro de Jacques de Saroug sur la Synagogue et l'Église." Also found in M. Albert, *Jacques de Serough, Homélies Contre les Juifs*, 160–81.

[36] See Albert, "Synagogue et l'Église, 144.

[37] See F. Graffin, "The Theme of Church as Bride in the Syriac Liturgies and Patristic Literature."

Path of the just on the way of the Son, preparing the way for the Son: 9–14.

Jacob walked along this path encouraged by the divine mysteries: 15–28.

He puts a stone under his head; the stone resembles the Church: 29–32.

2.   *Divine Revelations: 33–180*

Jacob's staff represents the Cross: 33–50.

Vision of a ladder combining heaven and earth and that only the soul can understand: 51–119.

Jacob is taught concerning hidden mysteries: 121–130.

Jacob sees the Son who encourages him to walk along his path: 131–142.

Not Isaac but the Lord who gave the blessing: 161–170.

Jacob awakens from the vision and is amazed: 180–192.

3.   *Jacob's Responses: 181–336*

Jacob asks to be blessed like Abraham and Isaac: 181–198.

From the vision Jacob understands that the Lord is on the mountain and so constructs a sanctuary: 193–202.

Jacob prefigures the Church by pouring oil over the cornerstone and thereby becomes a priest: 205–222.

The Son of God asks Jacob to anticipate His betrothal with the Church: 220–230; making Jacob's betrothal to a woman from Haran dependent on this: 220–235.

Jacob does as the Lord asked him, he builds the house of the Lord, to serve as a resting place when the Lord descends from heaven: 250–260.

Jacob perceives that God would climb down on the ladder to earth: 260–270.

As the Apostles, Jacob asks for bread and garments: 280–288.

Jacob's plea for daily bread, i.e. the Lord's Prayer; Jacob received it during the vision on the mountain: 289–310.

"The vision replete with mystery was to Jacob like a <teacher>"; he began to pray the Lord's Prayer: 311–335.

On the Church and Rachel [#75]

Path of the Son: 1–18.

The journey of the Mighty One: 19–46.

Jacob's path: 47–85.

Jacob beheld the mystery of the Church in Rachel: 86–98.

Our Lord who came to the world from His Father: 99–112.

The mystery of the Church enables Jacob to move the stone <of sin>:113–134.

Here the entire type of our Lord was accomplished: 135–154.

Jacob made a covenant with Laban for Rachel: 155–167.

Laban conspired to cheat Jacob of Rachel: 168–202.

Morning came and Jacob discovers he has been cheated; having served for Rachel, Leah has been given him: 203–238.

Jacob and the Son of God; Leah and Rachel God calls all Nations into communion with Himself: 239–270.

Moses leads Leah out of Egypt: 271–304.

Mysteries in the house of Laban – in Jacob our Lord was depicted and in Laban's daughter the Church: 305–324.

Jacob took the odious one as well as the one adorned with beauty, thus resembling our Lord who betrothed the Nation and the Nations to His Gospel: 325–330.

Text and Translation

HOMILY 74: A HOMILY ON JACOB'S REVELATION AT BETHEL

I. LOVE AS A PRINCIPLE OF EXEGESIS[1]

Dear is instruction spoken discreetly,
but dearer still when men hearken with love.[2]
Love alone possesses an ear that tries every word,
and it grows not weary whenever it inclines to listen.
5   One must attend to the histories of the righteous with love,
for it was also through love that they drew nigh unto God.
The world is odious to those who love righteousness,
and all other loves are vanquished by love that is of God.
It was not difficult for them to change their countries,

---

[1] Divisions of the Homily as suggested by Graffin have been followed. See Graffin, "Mimro de Jacques de Sarug," 226.

[2] Love (*ḥûbâ*): on divine love, Brock says that God's boundless love is a central theme throughout Syriac tradition from Ephrem to Isaac the Syrian, see Brock, *Spirituality*, 84. According to Bou Mansour, the centrality of divine love in Jacob's teaching is understudied and may be the most profound intuition of his work, see Bou Mansour, *Théologie de Jacques de Saroug* I, 31–33. Jacob situates love not in the divine will which might imply creation out of necessity but in the divine essence (*'îtûtâ*). He sees divine mercy as the source of Creation, Salvation and Incarnation. Jacob says human love is the only adequate response to God's love. It is also divine love that empowers human love in the understanding of Scripture. Elsewhere Jacob calls love a mediary (*meṣ'âyâ*): "It is right that love should stand now as a mediary, for without love the hearer has no understanding." See Brock, *Veil on Moses' Face*, lines 19–20. And see Hansbury, "Love as an Exegetical Principle."

TEXT AND TRANSLATION

10	for the Lord is the land of all the righteous and to Him did they make their way.
	By the mysteries[3] of the Son they were made exceedingly rich,
	and through their likeness to Him[4] they became known in diverse lands.
	By their deeds their revelations were made to shine forth,
	and by their visions their works were perfected.
15	On the great path of the Son of God they set out and proceeded,
	and each one of them made there a smooth passage.
	These mysteries drove forth the righteous Jacob from his place,
	so that he should go down and journey on the path of the Son from the moment he arrived.
	Isaac sent him forth laden with his blessings,
20	so that he should explore the mysteries of His path and then return to his land.
	He reached a place to pass the night and the mystery restrained him, that he should journey with it,
	although he knew not what he represented on the path which he had taken.
	The place on the mountain seemed so desolate to him that he feared to remain there alone,
	he even supposed that the Lord Himself was absent.

---

[3] Mysteries (*râzê*): symbols, signs.
[4] Lit., 'His likeness'.

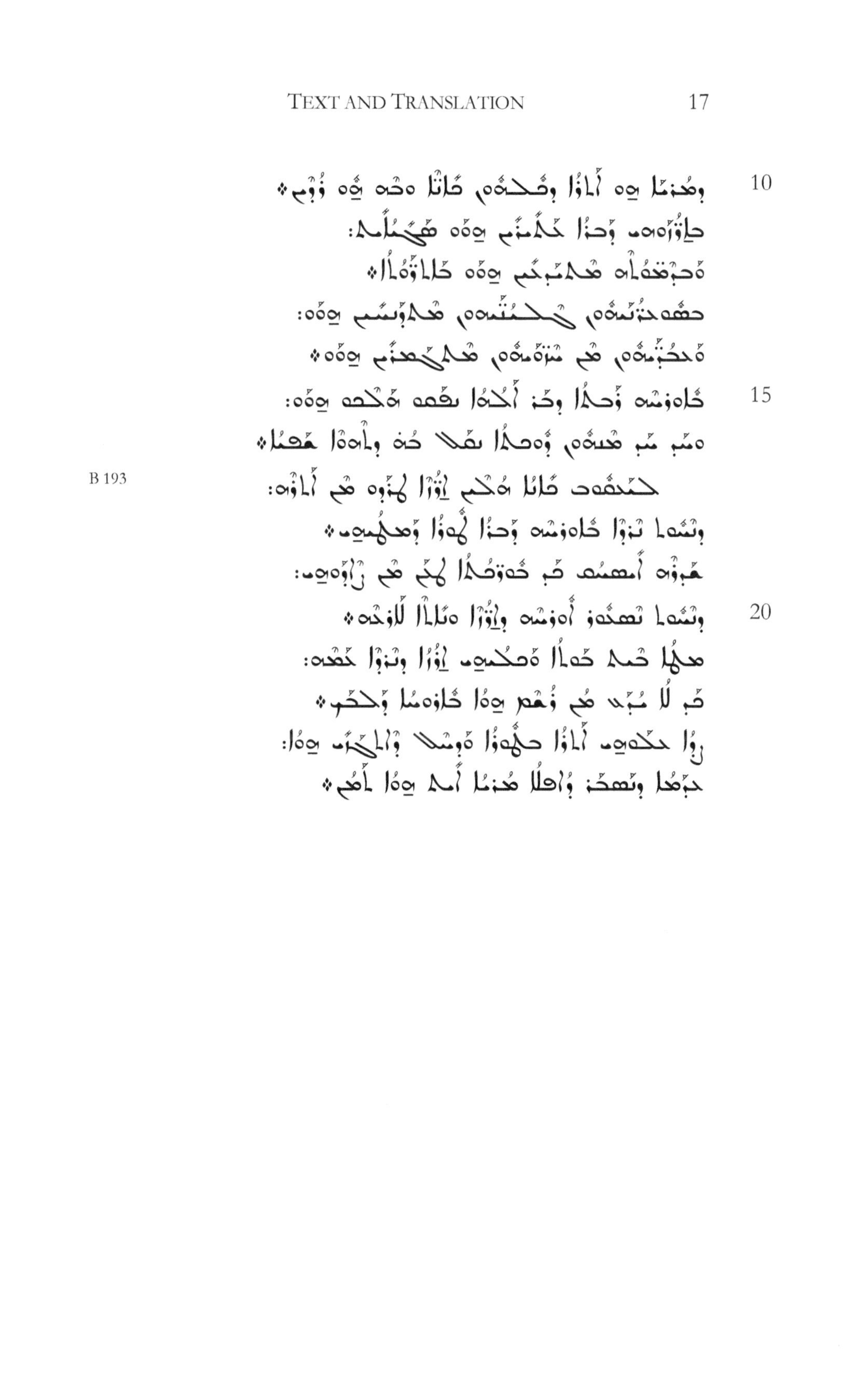

B 193

25	His mind succumbed to terror on the mountain and he fell asleep,
	a sleep whereby was depicted the symbol of the death of the Son of God.

- 25 His mind succumbed to terror on the mountain and he fell asleep,
  a sleep whereby was depicted the symbol of the death of the Son of God.
  There he feared that he would undergo suffering from diverse causes,
  for this path cannot be accomplished except through suffering.
  Taking up a stone, the righteous man placed it as a pillow and fell asleep,
- 30 for the mystery of the Son does not proceed without the Church.
  With this act Jacob began the path that he undertook,
  so that he should not even pass one night on his way without types.[5]

II. Divine Revelations

1. The Staff and the Cross

As soon as he went forth from his father's house, mysteries proceeded him,
and on that path[6] they descended with him and ascended like merchants.
- 35 He took a staff with him as he descended on his way,
so that the Cross of the Son should thereby be truly portrayed.
Who betrothed a wife with a staff, if not Jacob,
who in setting out took naught else with him save this?
This staff furnished his entire marriage gift for his brides,

---

[5] Types (*tûpsê*).

[6] On the imagery of the 'way' or 'path' (*ûrḥâ*), see Kollamparampil, "Divine Pedagogy," p. 87: "Adam is an image of the invisible Only-Begotten, and when he attains his goal, he attains the full likeness of the Only-Begotten…Adam's growth to perfection in, through and with Christ, is the foundation of this imagery of 'the way' that depicts the stages of revelation, the patterns of human behavior, the story of salvation…in a symbolic manner." See also Rilliet, "La métaphore du chemin."

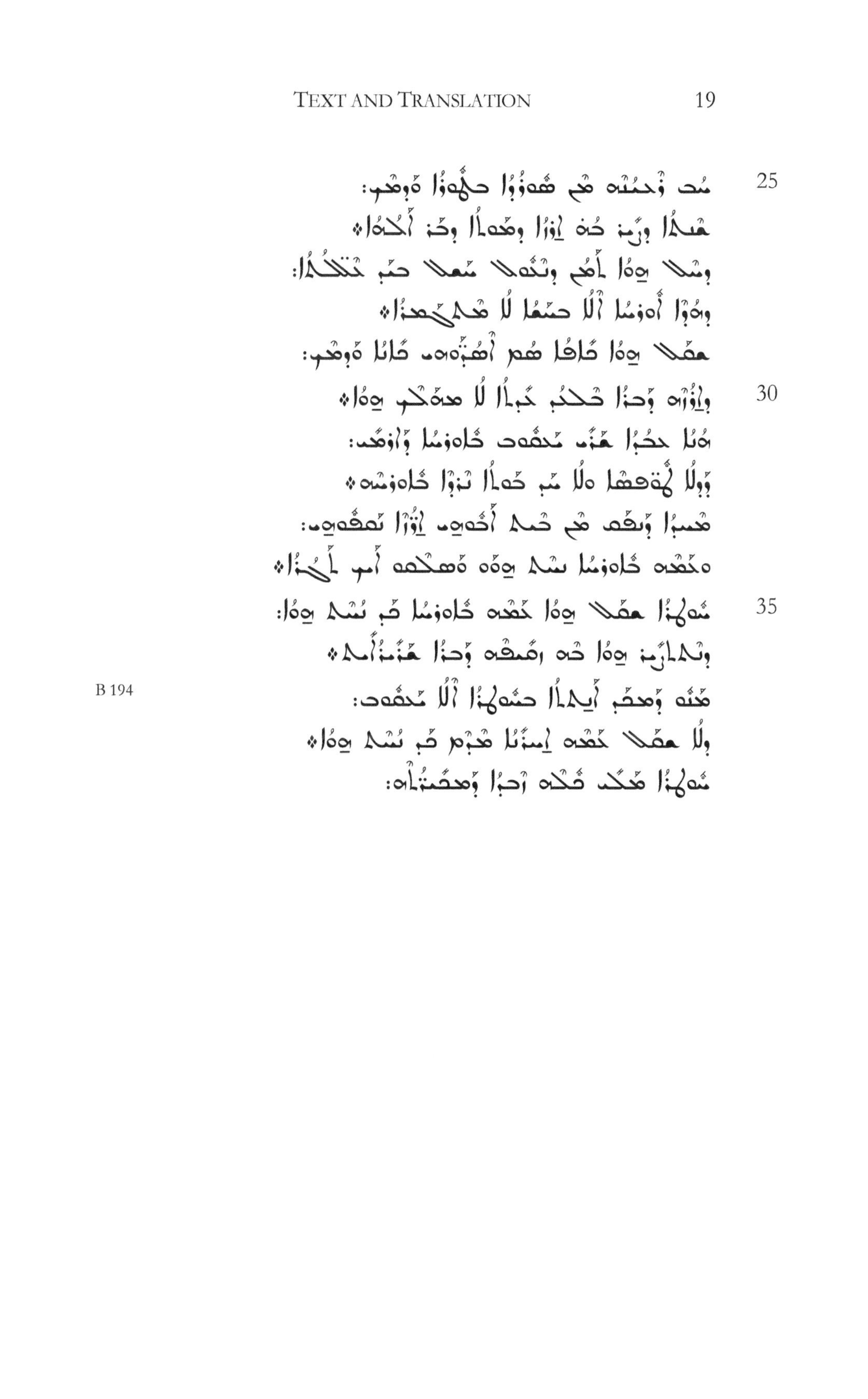

B 194

40   and by it he guarded from injury the sheep which he tended.
By it he drove off the savage beast from his flock,
and in it he found a companion for his way and riches in his sojourn.
The Cross alone has shone forth the Son of God to the world,
and it caused all riches to pour forth from Him upon created things.
45   Hereby the Church of the Nations,[7] the abandoned one, was betrothed;
hereby Satan and death were put to flight like thieves.
Jacob took its mystery when he descended to Haran,
and for this reason his path was more sublime than other paths.
He slumbered upon his staff and placing the stone as a pillow he fell asleep,
50   even as the Son espoused the Church and died upon the Cross.[8]

2. The Ladder and the Cross

Now when that sleep <replete> with mysteries settled upon the just man,
a dream opened heaven and came down to speak with him.
Heavenly powers in their legions encircled <Jacob>,
so as to accompany him during that descent so filled with wonder.[9]

---

[7] On 'Church and the Nations' in Ephrem see: Murray, *Symbols of Church and Kingdom*, 41–68. And see: Ephrem, *Commentary on Genesis* XXVI.3: "In the rock the mystery of the church is also represented, for it is to her that the vows and offerings of all the nations were soon to come." See note # 24 on stone (*kêphâ*).

[8] See Joshua, *Church as Bride of Christ*.

[9] Wonder (*tehrâ*): not simply an emotion brought on by what surpasses expectation or experience but a way of seeing, perceiving and feeling divine realities. As an integral part of revelation (*gelyânâ*) it occurs very often in Jacob of Serug. In his homily "On the Nativity of Our Lord," there are thirteen occurrences of *tehrâ* and thirteen of *dumrâ*. See also his homily "On the Name Wondrous that Our Lord Was Called." And see Hansbury, "Insight without Sight," for the importance of *temhâ/tehrâ* in later Syriac tradition.

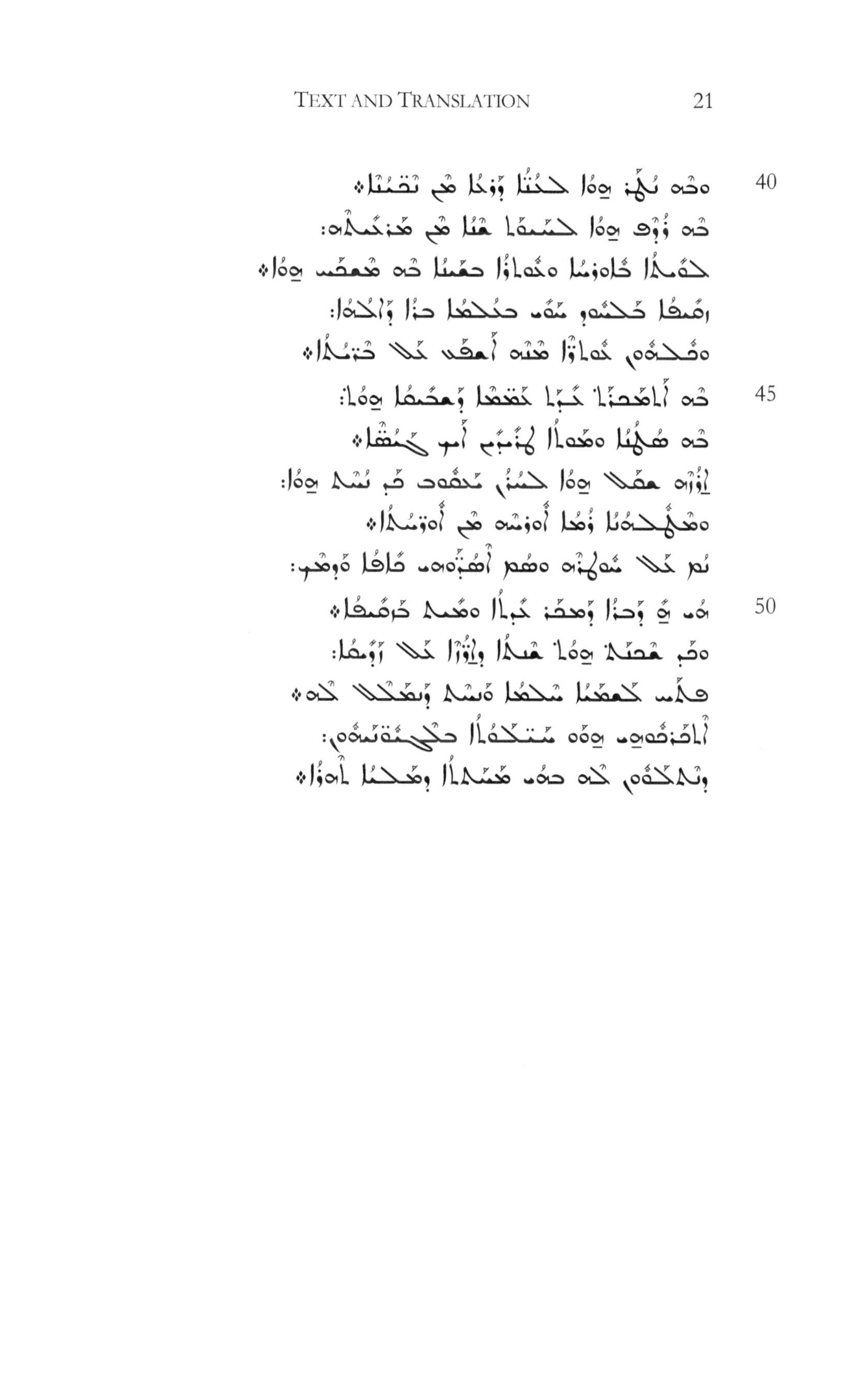

55   He took the image[10] of the Son so as to raise it up when He descended,
and the Watchers[11] cleaved to Him so as to better follow Him.
The legions came forth to glorify the King when He passed by,
so that He should not go without honor in this desolate place of His sojourn.
From humility Jacob called himself a poor man,
60   but the angels cried out at his descent: it is the King!
They beheld him how he embraced his staff and fell asleep upon the mountain peak,
and their assemblies encompassed him to gaze upon the image of the Crucifixion.
Now he saw in his dream that a ladder was set upon the earth
and its summit reached even unto Heaven, a great wonder!
65   Not a single one save Jacob had seen this new spectacle,
this stupefying vision so replete with veracious types.
Who has seen a ladder like this one, from the ages,
which was placed on earth and reached unto Heaven, who save Jacob?
He beheld angels ascending thereby so as to mount on high,
70   and also other ranks descending thereby towards terrestrial beings.
Behold, an ascent that is awesome to the one who beholds it,
for heaven and earth draw nigh, the one to its companion.
May the soul be filled with wonder here at this mighty vision
and thus be opened to the narration about this revelation!

---

[10] Image (*salmâ*).
[11] I.e., the angels.

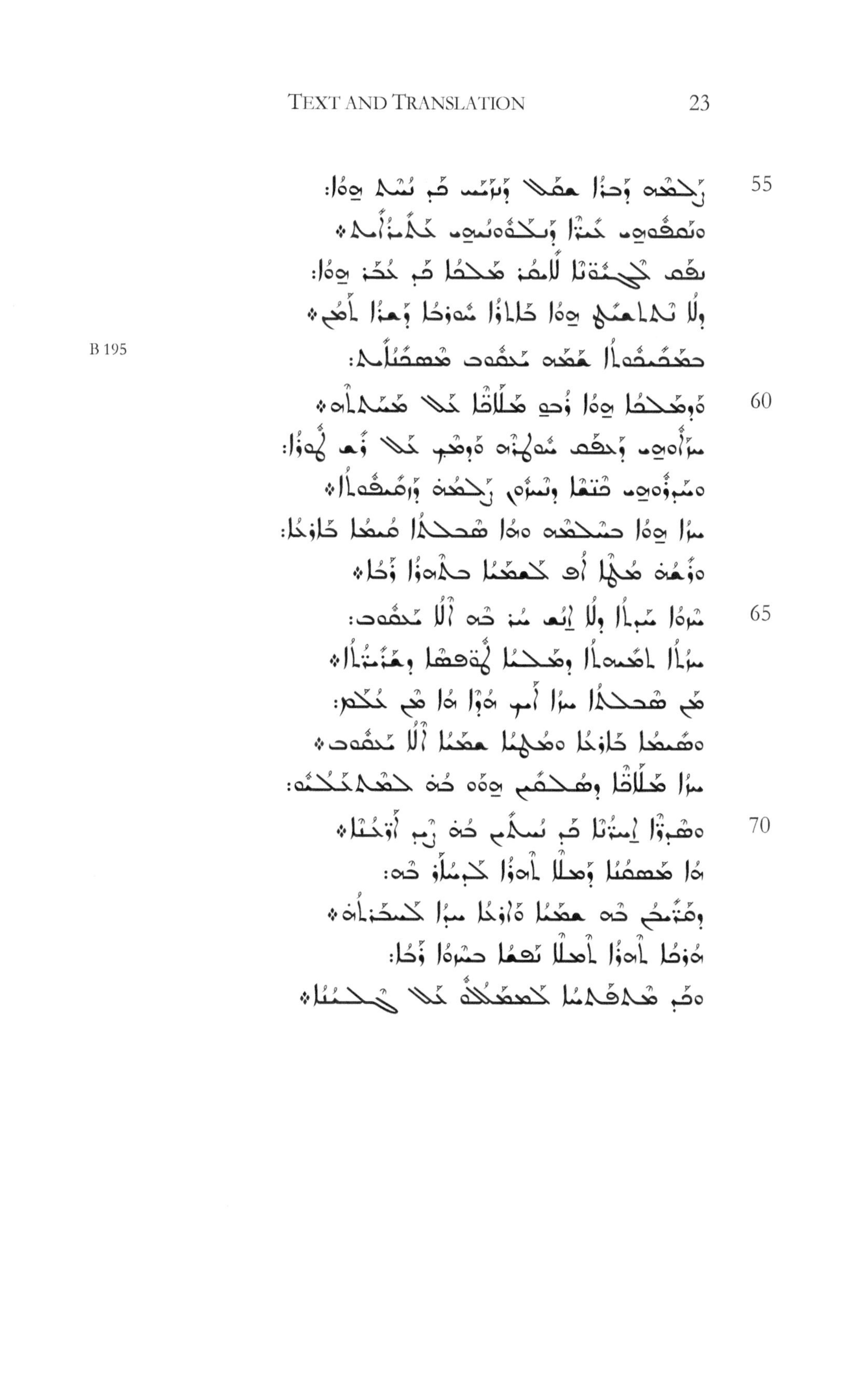

75 For speech is barren if it does not originate from the motions of the soul,
and its force is weakened when it is not pronounced with love.
That which the soul beholds she may speak when it is needful,
but from mere report she should not attempt to make such tidings known.
May her vision be filled with revelations whenever they appear
80 and when she is prepared for the narration of their visitations!
Let us not recite Jacob's revelation like a fable,
rather let us deliver up our souls to this vision and thus examine it!
Think not that it was a mere ladder which you hear of in the reading,
but understand something else by this and you shall have the explanation.
85 Now if angels ascend on it, why is it a ladder,
for why should steps be set in array for these spiritual beings?
Here the very mystery[12] explains itself,
for the path of the Son was made visible by this ladder.
The Cross was set up like an awesome ladder,
90 and thereby man was truly raised on high.
Through the birth of the Son the angels descended towards earthly creatures
and humanity ascends from out of the abyss into the celestial regions.
By the Cross, heaven and earth which were at enmity, were again united,
and peace reigned between the two that were once divided.

---

[12] Mystery (*râzâ*): the use of the term 'mystery' refers not to some esoteric doctrine but to divine economy. See Golitzin, "Image and Glory," 338–39. As noted by Golitzin, Bondi interprets this as esoteric doctrine rather than divine economy (*madabbrânûtâ*). See Bondi, *Three Monophysite Christologies*, 128–31. See also Golitzin, 324–30, for other comments on the re-evaluation of Jacob's "Mythology" as rather themes of classical Christian preaching.

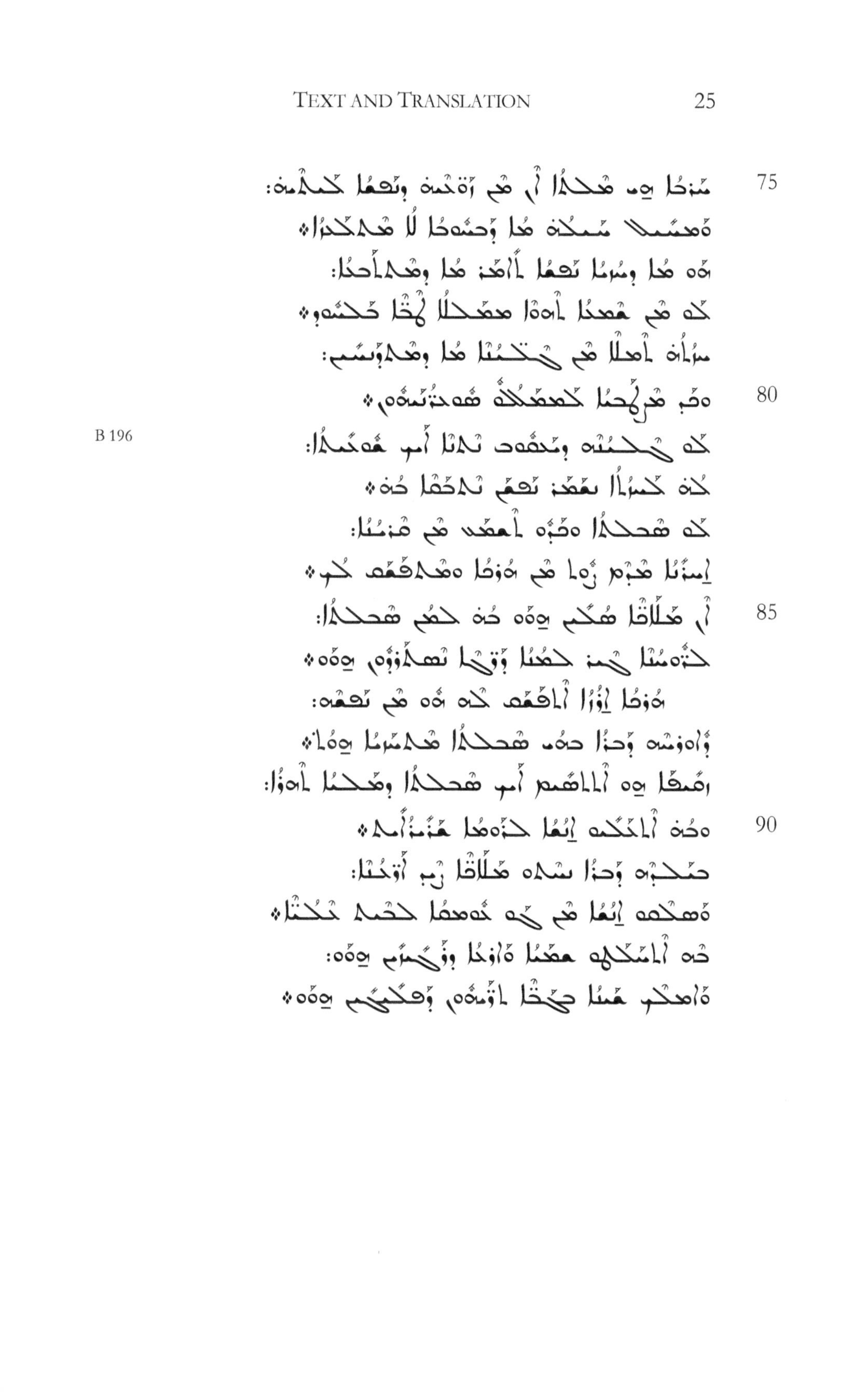

95	The Cross stood on the earth like a ladder having many steps,
	and extended itself so that by it all earthly beings could rise up.
	By its power the Cross has broken through the middle wall of enmity,[13]
	and when it was lifted up it joined terrestrial creatures with the celestial ones.
	The Cross carried and raised up humanity to be exalted on high,
100	and it drew and brought down the Watchers[14] to sing praises in the lower regions.
	As a result, the celestial powers rushed forth and descended,
	so as to behold the awesome wonder that was hidden from their ranks.
	To the Cross peoples and generations look, that they might climb to the realm on high,
	for it is both smooth and easy to ascend and descend thereby.
105	Gaze upon the Cross and fill your eyes with its grandeur,
	for it is a spacious path unhindered from its course!
	It is like a staircase between earthly and heavenly beings,
	And if did not exist, the one would never approach the other.
	Its way is easy to tread even for the departed;
110	it laid waste to Sheol and behold, even the dead ascend thereby!
	Who could ascend to Heaven without the aid of the Cross,
	and if it did not exist, what would have reconciled earth with Heaven?
	Who could tread down that lofty realm between the two,
	so as to unite the one side with the other, if it were not for the Cross?

---

[13] Cf. Eph. 2:14.

[14] Watchers: the Syriac tradition frequently designates angels as Watchers (Dan. 4:13,17). Watchers figure prominently in pseudepigraphic and later Jewish mystical literature. In Merkabah texts such as 3 Enoch, they are a separate order: "Above all these are four great princes called Watchers...their abode is opposite the throne of Glory...they receive glory from the glory of the Almighty and are praised with the praise." See 3 Enoch 28:1–3.

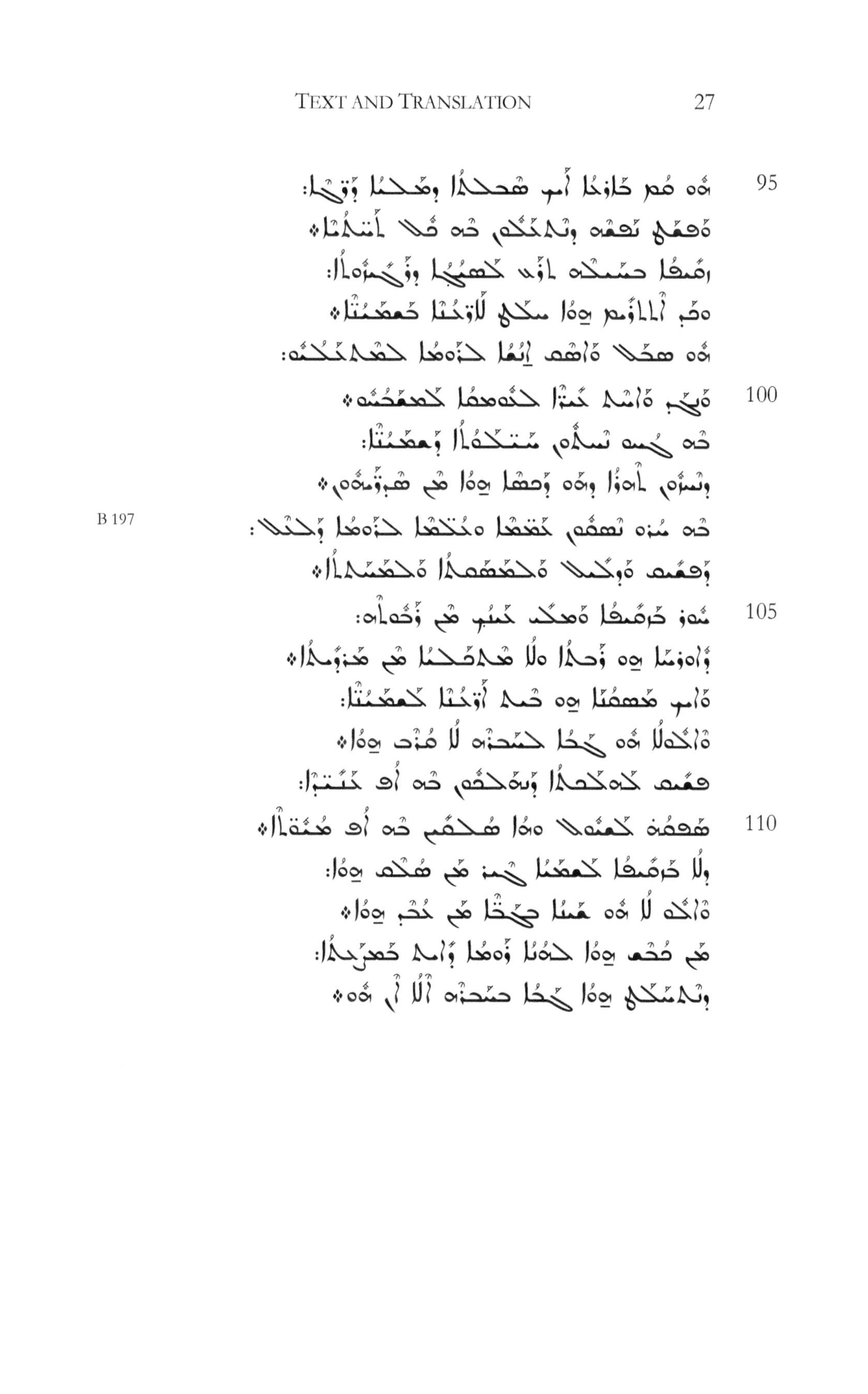

B 197

115   Who could have lifted up the thief into the Kingdom,[15]
unless the Cross had bent down to him to enable his journey?
What could have drawn forth the dead of Sheol from their tombs,
unless the Cross had gone down after them and raised them up?
This, therefore, is Jacob's vision and his revelation,[16]
120   and in that ladder he really beheld the Cross.
Now this dream was for Jacob a revealed writing,
and the vision permitted him to read in his sleep and thereby be enlightened.
In the quiet of the night he rested from the turbulence of the world and he beheld
the Lord of the ages teaching him concerning hidden things.
125   He entered into sleep and reached the realm of things mystical and secret,
and there he learned hidden mysteries and their interpretations.
He slept, it is said, upon the earth, but he was vigilant for revelations,
for he beheld a wonder, being undisturbed by created things.
Sleep closed his outward eyes to things visible,
130   and the vision came and opened wide his soul to things hidden.
He saw the Cross standing upon the earth like a ladder
and how it became a pathway whereon the celestial powers travelled.
Above it he beheld the Lord standing as He who orders all,
and He encouraged Jacob to wend his way with a steady step.

---

[15] Cf. Eph. 2:14.

[16] Revelation (*gelyânâ*): according to Ephrem, creation itself is revelatory. Nature, the O.T. and the N.T. are sources of revelation. See Beggiani, "Early Syriac Theology," 26–40. Ephrem understands creation as revelatory because it was created by the Word Himself. The Bible contains revelatory symbols of Christ because creation does. See also Murray, "Theory of Symbolism," 3 ff.

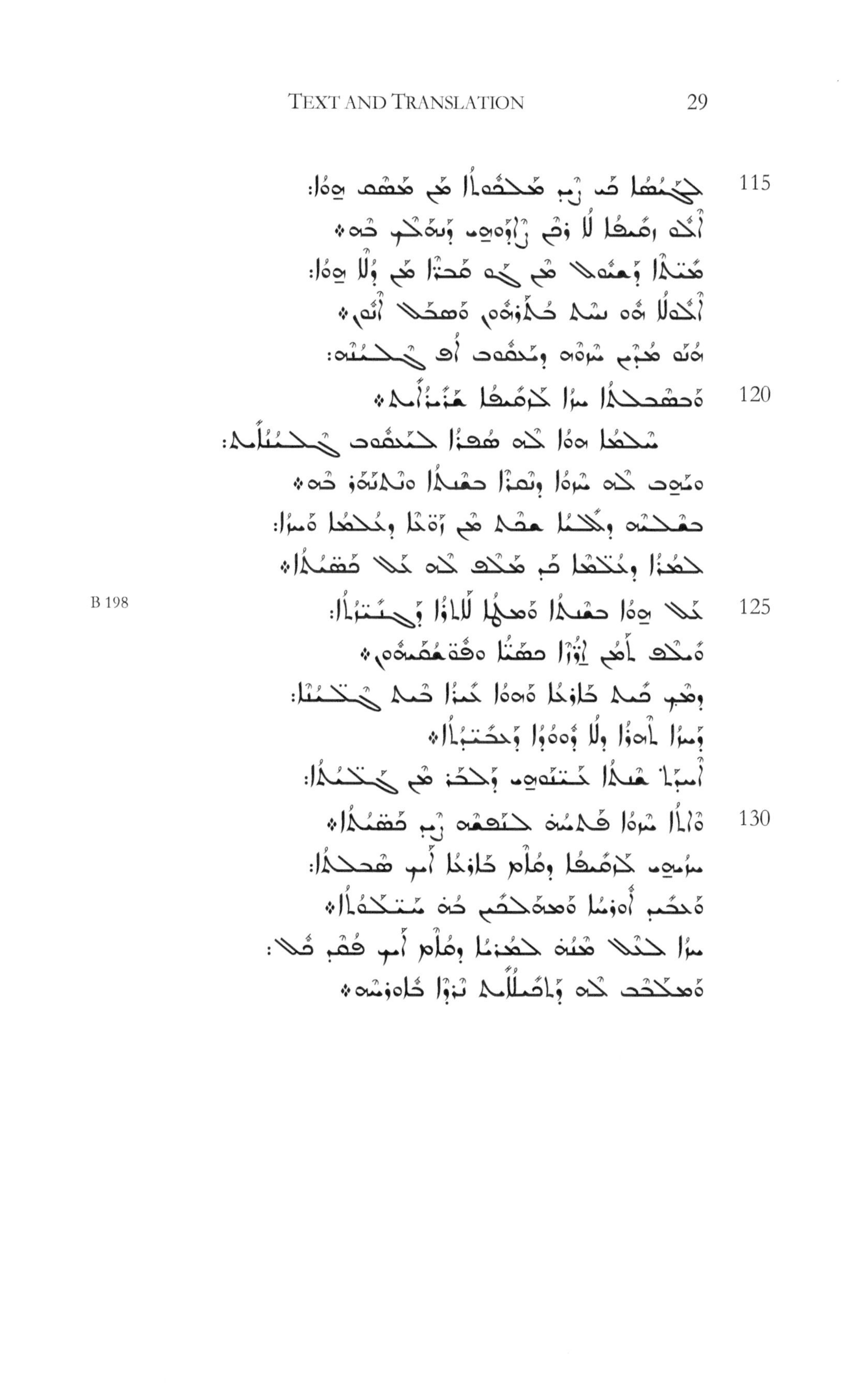

B 198

135   I am the Lord and God of Abraham your father,
      I am the God of Isaac, and with you I will be.
      This land I give to you and you shall be its master,
      and your seed shall inherit these regions and their habitations.
      In you all nations shall be blessed and through your seed,
140   and you shall multiply upon the earth and through the Nations you
            shall possess the four quarters of the world.
      I am with you; whom, then, will you fear upon your journey?
      I am your guardian and who can bring you low?[17]
      At this place the Lord gave Jacob provisions for his way,
      so that he should lack nothing in a land that was not his own.
145   The beholding of the mystery – for he was worthy to gaze upon
            it –
      brought riches to impart to him, lest poverty should vex him.
      He went before a king and as a present he received blessings,
      for he journeyed so as to depict[18] in other lands the image of beau-
            tiful things.
      By the crucifixion the young Jacob was blessed,

---

[17] Cf. Gen. 28:13–15.

[18] Depict (*ṣûr*): Jacob like Ephrem speaks of types and symbols (*râzê*) as being depicted or drawn in Scripture. In Ephrem, "God or Christ is the artist who in the Scriptures has painted pictures of the whole economy of salvation in the words and deeds of the prophets and the apostles," see Griffith, "Image of the Image Maker." See also Jacob's "On the Mysteries, Types and Figures of Christ," with its extensive visual terminology: depict, figure, represent, made an image, draw, trace, skilled painter, resemblance, carve an image, color, imprint, resemble, etc. See J. Konat, "Metrical Homily." (Konat does have issues with Jacob's authorship of the homily, at least in part).

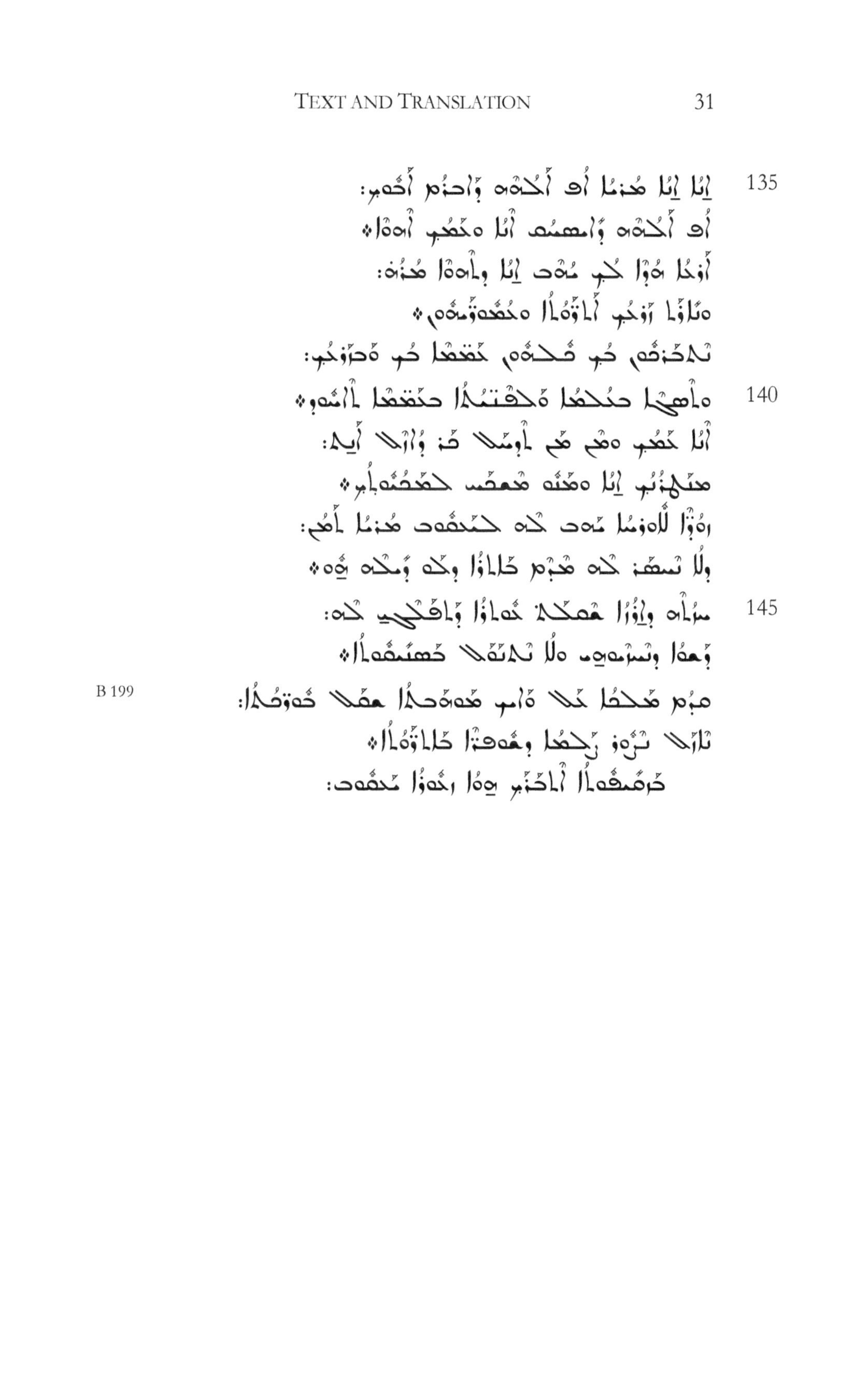

B 199 :

150	for from it great salvation would be shed forth upon all the world.
	"The Nations of the earth will be blessed through your seed," but not he through the Nations,
	for it says, "The Nations of the earth shall be blessed through you and through your seed."[19]
	Behold, from that very time, the Nations received this blessing,
	and when the gracious Jacob was blessed, the blessing settled upon them.
155	Through him and through his seed the Nations of the earth were blessed;
	then let that Nation be silent which vaunts itself above pagans!
	All the peoples are blessed by God
	through this revelation which was the Crucifixion's type.
	The mystery of the Son poured forth these blessings richly,
160	and it gave hope lovingly unto all the Nations.
	It was not Isaac but the Lord who gave the blessing,
	who caused both young and old to be equal by His word.
	Behold, from that very time He blessed all the Nations together,
	for the mystery of the Son was sufficient to bless them all.
165	But if it was not His mystery which shone forth in that place,
	for what cause was the Lord manifest upon the ladder?
	The righteous man beheld the Cross upon the mountain and the Lord upon it,
	for by the Cross the Nations of the earth received the blessing.
	The Cross, replete with mysteries, was fixed into the mountain like a ladder,[20]

---

[19] Gen. 28:14.

[20] Cross as bridge (*gaśrâ*): because of the chasm (*peḥtâ*) separating creation from the Creator a bridge is necessary. Koonammakkal clarifies: "Ephrem's idea of ontological chasm is only a corollary of the semitic concept of God being absolutely unique rather than indicating a spatial divide." See Koonammakkal, *Theology of Divine Names*, 147. On other aspects of the Cross and its redemptive relation to the Church, see Beggiani, *Early Syriac Theology*, 55–76. The ladder (*sebelṭâ*) which appears here reappears at the Resurrection, see Kollamparampil, *Select Festal Homilies*, p. 322.

TEXT AND TRANSLATION

B 200

170   and He stood at its summit and by it blessed all the peoples.
         But if, in truth, it is not really as I say,
           why was it necessary for the Lord to reveal Himself upon the ladder?
         It is plainly evident that this \<ladder\> was the Cross,
         for the Lord was upon it and by it all the Nations were blessed.
175   He stretched out his word so that not just one Nation should be blessed thereby,
         but all of them, and truly He was able to give His blessing unto all.
         In a mystery the Cross is set up here like a ladder,
         and for the Nations it was like a staircase unto God.
         The righteous man was awestruck at the new vision that was shown him;
180   the just man was awakened and set aflame because of his revelation.

III. Jacob's Responses

1. Request of Blessings

         A great light shone forth in his soul through this new spectacle,
         and by revelations, as it were by fire, he was enkindled.
         He heard from the Lord the name of Abraham and Isaac,
         and he was aroused with sore longing, for by this list his genealogy was mentioned.
185   More earnestly, then, did he pray making this supplication:
         "I entreat You, my Lord, place my name now along with these.
         In this list grant me a place after my father Isaac;
         say: 'And the God of Jacob,' and I shall be joined with my fathers.
         Not 'of Abraham and of Isaac' only, but 'of Jacob' too,

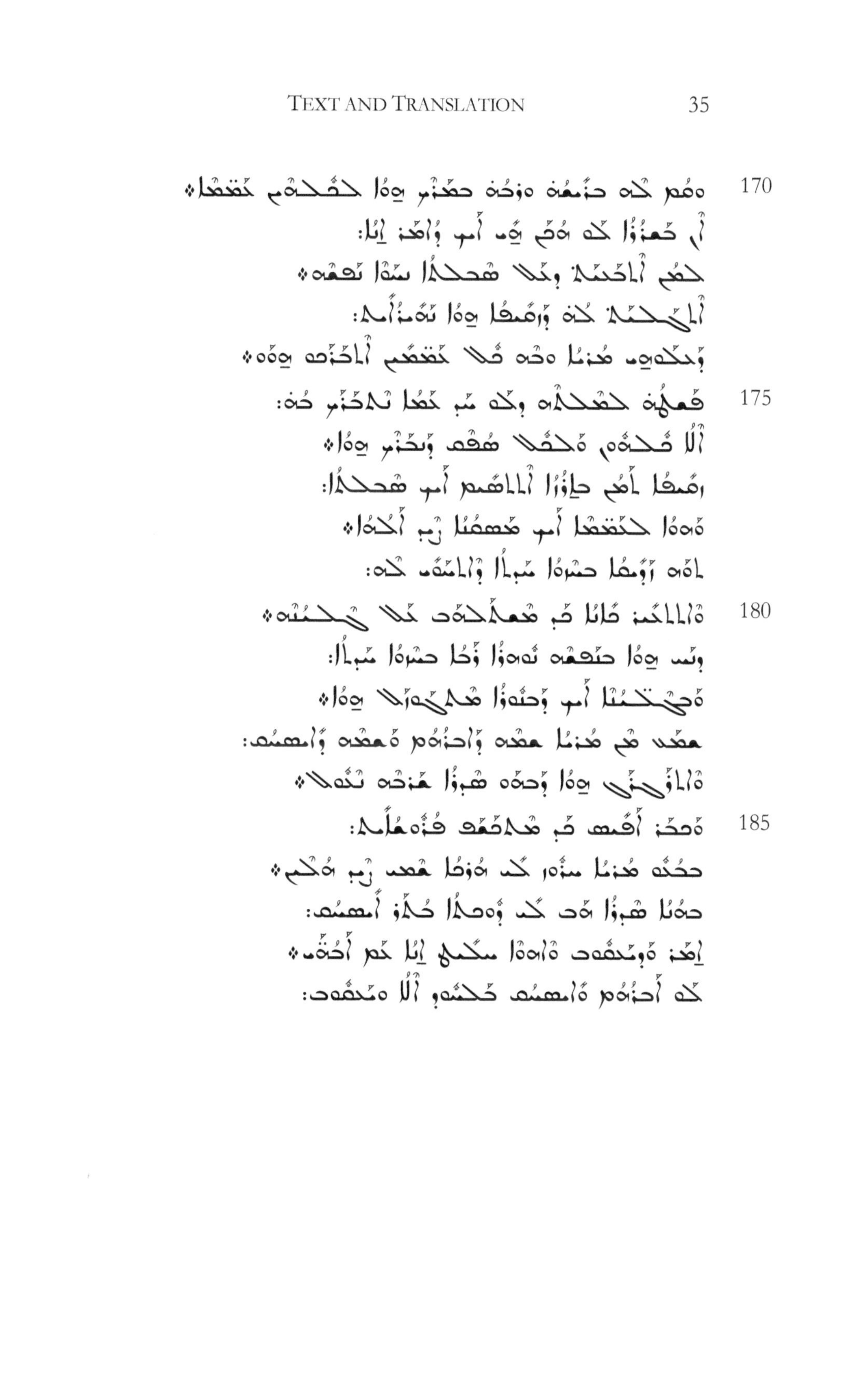

190   add on my name after theirs, for this is my ardent desire.
      Into this chain of their names may I enter when You repeat it;
      number me with them and in this enumeration I shall have a good name!"
      Jacob was illumined by the revelation which spoke with him,[21]
      for that mighty vision during sleep inflamed him greatly.
195   "Truly," he said, "the Lord is in this place[22]
      and I knew it not until now through this wonder which I behold."
      "This is the house of God," he said, "truly indeed,
      and this is the gate of Heaven in all certainty."[23]

2. Placing of the First Stone of the Church

      He fell asleep a poor man but he rose up rich from the revelation,
200   in the evening he was an exile from the land where at night he became the master.
      In the morning he arose and began the construction of the Church,
      so as to honor the place of his vision with the beauty of mysteries.
      He erected there a stone[24] and brought forth oil which he poured upon its crest,

---

[21] Alfeyev, in the context of later Syriac writers notes that: "Revelation (*gelyânâ*) refers to the inner contiguity of a person with an unearthly reality; it does not necessarily presuppose seeing a certain visible image." See Alfeyev, *Spiritual World of Isaac the Syrian*, 229–36.

[22] Place (*atrâ*): the term 'place' occurs in scriptures often associated with theophany and with the tabernacle/temple. On the use in Rabbinic thought of *maqom*/place, as divine name denoting God's omnipotence and on occasion overlapping with shekinah, see Urbach, *Sages*, 66–79.

[23] Cf. Gen. 28:16,17.

[24] Stone (*kêphâ*): see Ephrem's, *Commentary on Genesis* XXVI, 2-3: "In the oil that<Jacob> poured upon the stone, he was depicting the mystery of Christ who was hidden inside it…In the rock (*kêphâ*) the mystery of the church is also represented, for it is to her that the vows and offerings of all the nations were soon to come." See also *Commentary on the Diatessaron* XXI, 21: "A stone was placed at the entrance to the tomb…this [stone], on which the angel was sitting, [had to keep guard] over that which Jacob had placed under his head" guarding "the gate of our Lord." At the resurrection there was an earthquake and the mystery of the Church emerging

B 201

---

from the tomb " introduced the Gentiles into the Church": the centurion being the first witness to the resurrection. Cf. Matt. 27:54. See Murray, *Symbols of Church and Kingdom*, 205–238.

so that all the types[25] of the Church should be accomplished clearly.
205 O Jacob, what are you doing on this path which you have undertaken,
why and in what manner is oil [needed] for the stone?
Who, then, has shown you to do this astonishing deed
and why do you so reverently give honor to this stone?
Who has taught you to anoint a stone here on this mountain,
210 for no man has done such a thing from the ages, besides you!
A new work has Jacob wrought upon this mountain,
a work the like of which had not been performed before him.
Abraham did not teach him to anoint the stone with oil,
nor from Isaac did he receive this new thing that he did.
215 Being enlightened in his soul by the awesome revelation that he saw,
from then he began to perform that great work in the world.
The mighty vision made the righteous Jacob a priest,
and with that which there was at hand he took up the work of anointing.
The spectacle of the mystery poured light upon his thoughts,
220 so that he did there properly that which was needful to do.
He built God a house in the name that he gave before setting up the stone,
so that one might say with certain knowledge that this was the Church in the world.
He called the entire place with discernment "The House of God,"[26]
and he set up therein a stone and anointed it as in a mystery.

---

[25] Types (*túpsê*).
[26] Gen. 28:19.

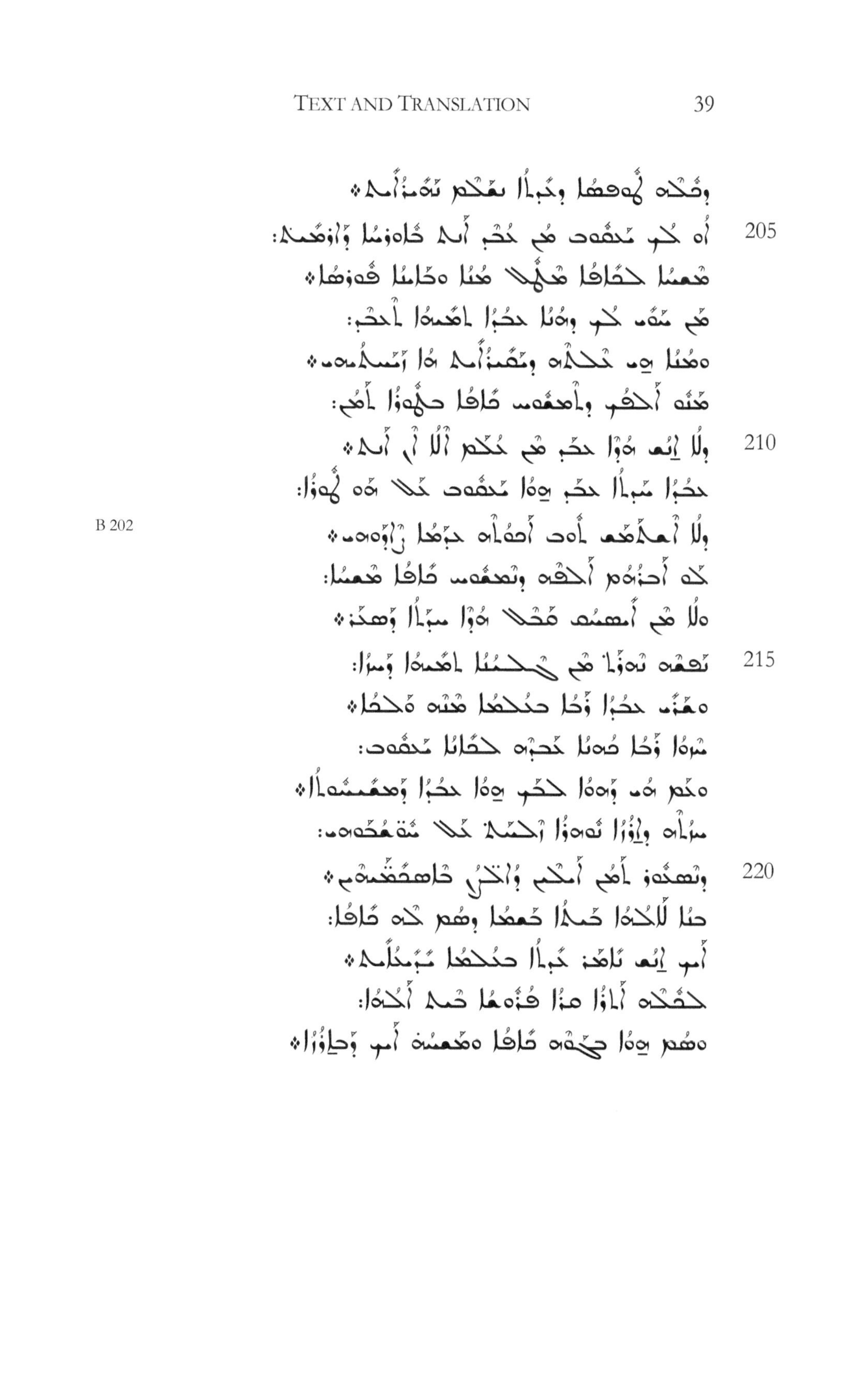

225   The Cross descended so as to affect the contract of betrothal,[27]
but without the oil its word could not be certain.
The type of the Son shone forth in a dream upon that discerning man,
and when he was awakened, he depicted for Him a worthy image.[28]
The revelation descended and stopped him on the path as he was journeying,
230   that he should not pass on until he had betrothed the Church unto the Son.
"Accomplish what pertains to Me," He said, "and thereafter go about your business,
engrave for Me the types and then go and seek your own affairs!
Make here for Me a mystical marriage feast through this new vision,
and thereafter take a wife pleasing to your soul, for she is also a symbol!"[29]
235   Betroth the Church to Me, and then you shall be betrothed to the daughter of Haran,[30]
build a house for Me, and then pursue your own affairs!
But if the daughter of the King is not betrothed mystically,
then neither will your path attain its goal successfully.
Make for Me a marriage contract with the Church and go your way,
240   walking on the path in which all the mysteries are portrayed!
Raise up a memorial of your vision upon the mountain and then depart,
lest the sight of that mystery should slip away from your mind!
Bring oil and pour it over the stone, which is the Church,
and represent her for Me, for after a time she shall be restored!

---

[27] See Beggiani, *Early Syriac Theology*, 60.

[28] Image (*salmâ*).

[29] Symbol (*râzâ*).

[30] See Beggiani, *Early Syriac Theology*, 60: "Jacob of Serugh offers a profound insight into the theology of marriage by seeing in every marriage of man and woman a reflection of the mystery of the wedding of church to Christ." See also the work of S.K. Joshua (forthcoming, Delhi).

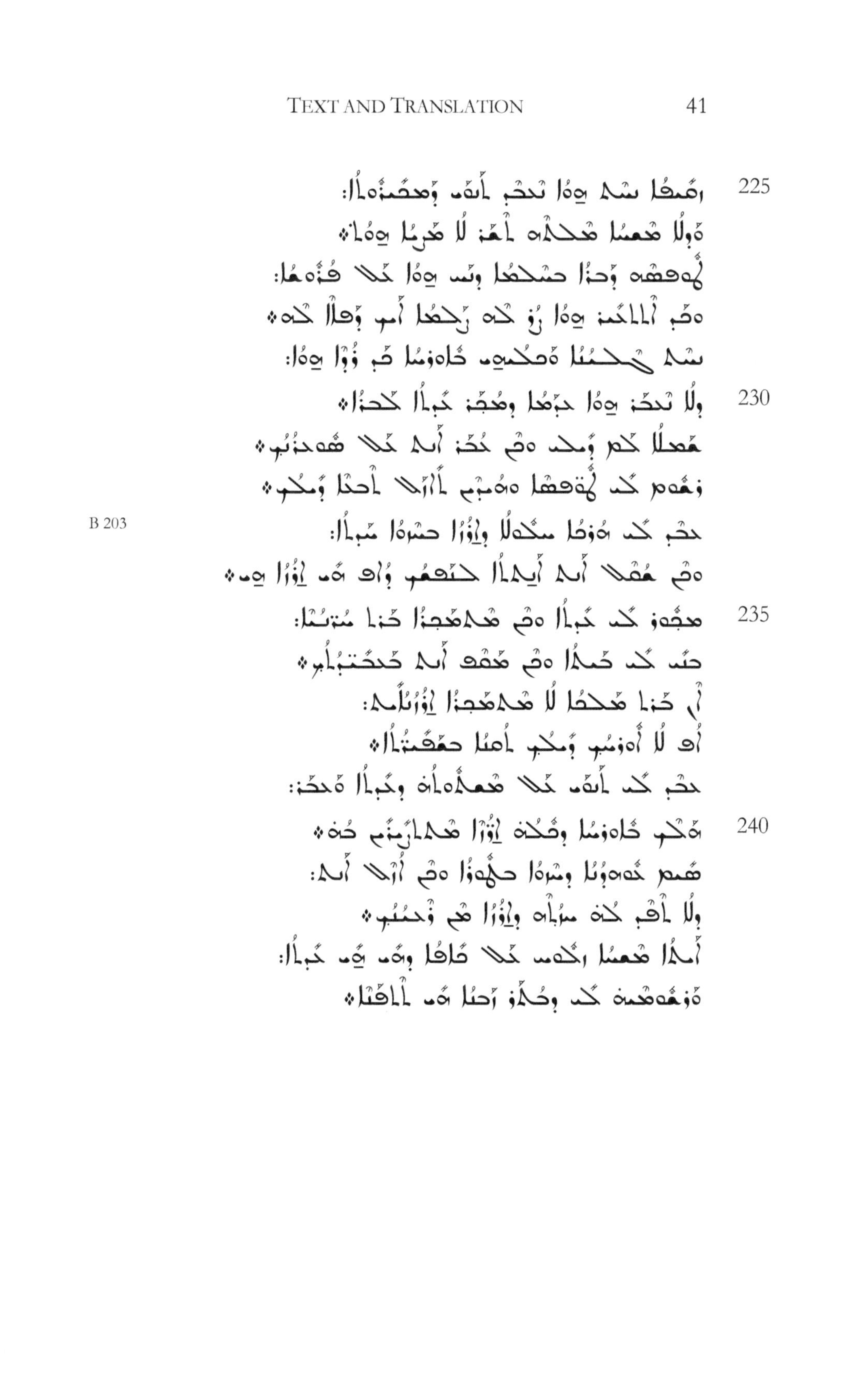

B 203

245   Lay a foundation for the great house of the King's bride,
so that there all the righteous will establish all their offspring!
Prepare for Me the bridal chamber, so that the mystery might enter and be celebrated there,
until I Myself make the great wedding feast throughout the whole world"!
Such beauty did Jacob behold through the revelation,
250   and he set up a stone and called the place 'the house of God.'
"The Lord is in this place," he said, "and I knew it not;
gate of Heaven is opened to the lower realm and I did not discern it."
He beheld the Lord, how He had set His face to descend unto the earth,
and he built a house for Him so as to make a resting place for His sojourn.
255   "Now," he said, "a place for His descent to earthly beings is prepared,
and the one realm that was at enmity with its comrade has now come to agreement with it.
The steps[31] which are in the middle realm tread down the lofty heights,
and the rugged place is made smooth by the choir of the Watchers.
The Lord, who stands on top of the ladder,[32] desires to descend:

---

[31] I.e., of the ladder.

[32] Jacob's *Prose Homily on the Nativity*: "Today, the revelation to Jacob is clearly explained: that same Lord who was standing at the summit of the ladder, behold, has descended to make human beings ascend to heaven." See Kollamparampil Par. 20, p. 135. See also *Prose Homily on the Sunday of the Resurrection*: "An awesome clamour of angels was heard from the air, a ladder of light was placed between the tomb and heaven, the one that had been seen by Jacob at Bethel; and the Lord was standing, not above it, ready to descend, but below it, ready to ascend." Par. 10, p. 322. Trans., Kollamparampil, *Select Festal Homilies*.

TEXT AND TRANSLATION

B 204

260 I shall make ready for Him a house that will be fit where He may be honored.
It is revealed to me that one day the Lord will descend to earth
and as a man will manifest Himself among earthly beings.
For if, truly, He was not indicating that He will come down,
for what reason did He stand upon the ladder, which has so many steps?
265 He has set His face to descend and to be with us,
and so I have built a house that will be ready for His glory, as it were.
He wishes that we should make an abode upon the earth, so that when He descends
His resting place will be prepared already, even from this moment.
Descending, He will surely descend, either sooner or later on,
270 therefore let the world learn from me that which even I knew not"!
As soon as Jacob received the revelation from God,
he began the work of truth in the world like an industrious man.
He depicted[33] the image of the great house by the rock which he set up,
and he sealed the mystery by the oil, so that it would shrine brightly.

3. Vows of Poverty and Renunciation

275 He completed his work and began to offer the vows of righteousness;
he traced[34] out the Church and set to making it steadfast through his prayers.

---

[33] Depicted (*ṣûrtā*).
[34] Traced (*rašâm*).

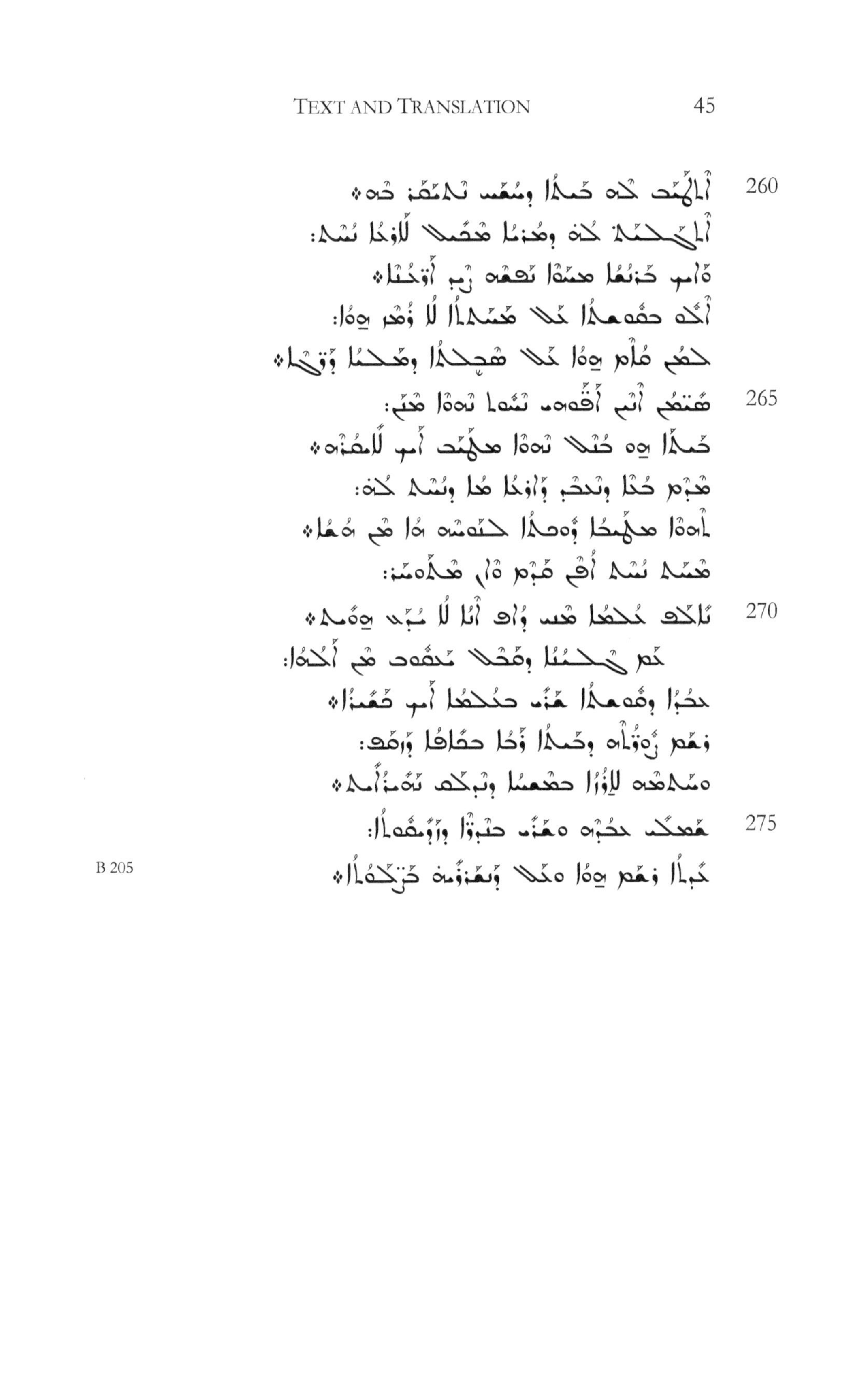

B 205

"If," he said, "God shall be with me wherever I am going,
He will give into my hands raiment to put on and bread to eat."[35]
Here also does the doctrine of the Son brilliantly shine forth,
for with the thinking of a poor man he began to wend his way.
He asked from God only for his food and raiment,
that in him there might be depicted the perfect path of apostleship.
If wealth were not superfluous to the prudent man,
he would not have sought for bread and raiment only.
If he sought for riches, he would not have fled away
nor would he have abandoned Abraham's possessions.
When he received the blessing, he ran off in pursuit of righteousness,
and his daily bread sufficed him to care for his every pleasure.

4. Jacob invokes the Our Father

In the Church which in a mystery Jacob built when fleeing,
behold, even from that time he prayed the prayer which our Lord has taught us.
"Give me always my daily bread," he entreated,
and for the same our Lord also enjoined the apostles to pray.
This prayer was also fitting for this path of Jacob's,
so that all the sayings of apostleship should be uttered.

---

[35] Cf. Gen. 28:20. Beginning of Jacob's reflection on the Our Father, see F. Siroli, "Jacob of Serugh and the Lord's Prayer." Mar Jacob sees in Jacob's request an anticipation of the Lord's Prayer. Siroli notes that Mar Jacob states "that Jacob the Patriarch recited in Bethel the Prayer that the Lord taught and commanded to be prayed by the apostles." See Siroli, 27–30.

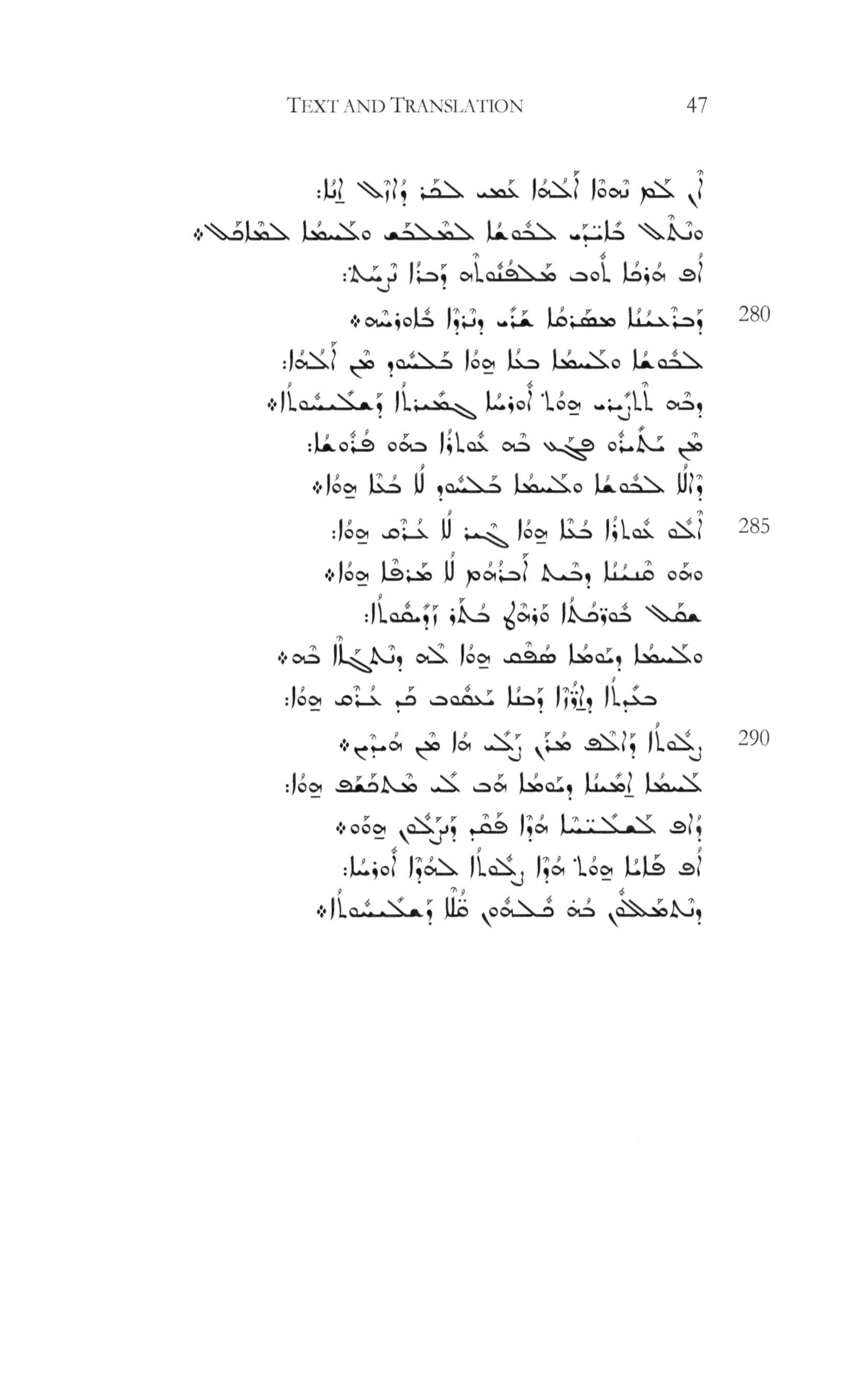

295 It is great wealth for one to possess his daily bread together with his God,
and if there be anything outside of this, it is superfluous to him.
Jacob took no thought for the morrow on the path which he undertook,
for sufficient unto the day is the evil thereof and the care concerning it.[36]
The path of the Crucifixion shone forth before the righteous one
300 and he gazed upon it and saw that his daily bread alone would be sufficient.
Until his soul had received enlightenment from the revelation,
he did not know the power of this prayer.
He prayed not thus when he left his father's house,
nor throughout the day while on the road did he learn it.
305 In the evening he laid down to sleep without uttering this prayer,
but when the revelation shone upon him during the night,[37] his soul was illumined.
He began to repeat the prayer commanded to the Lord's apostles,[38]
so that they should never seek more than for their daily bread.
He beheld how rich is the poverty of the Son
310 and went forth in pursuit of Him, so that through Him he might grow very rich.
The vision replete with mystery was to Jacob like a master,
for it instructed him on what to say when he stood in prayer.
He asked not for wealth, which is nothing to <those who discern>,[39]
but henceforth he sought for raiment and for bread according to his need.

---

[36] Cf. Matt. 6:34.
[37] See the comments of Alfeyev on 'revelation', note #21.
[38] Matt. 6:11; Luke 11:3.
[39] Lit. "to discerning men".

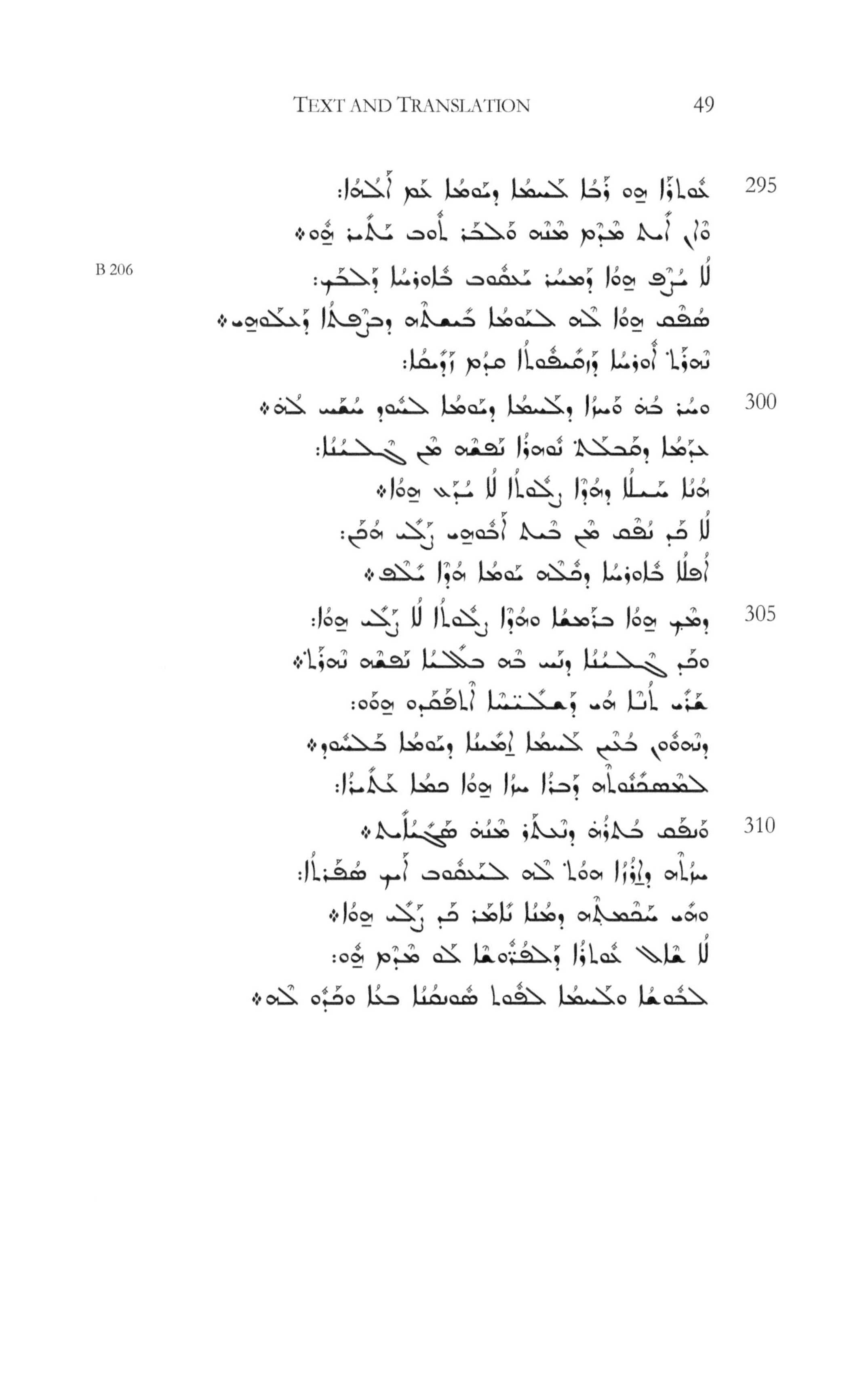

B 206

315	The intellect of the righteous yearns not for excesses,
	nor do they fill their souls with anxiety over vanities.
	That alone which is needful do they take from their possessions,
	even bread and raiment, and they are not made captive by desire.
	A simple life is rest for them, full of blessings,
320	and through its toil they magnify their wisdom.
	The covetous one is slain by his daily cares for many things,
	although he is unable during one day to live for the one to come.
	Tomorrow's bread is superfluous to you throughout today,
	even as that of yesterday is of no use to you at all.
325	But if each day you seek to accomplish only what is necessary,
	you will not during one day worry yourself with the cares of many days.
	"Sufficient unto the day," He says, "is the evil thereof and the care concerning it,"
	and this without a doubt suffices one for his entire life.
	Therefore Jacob asked for raiment and bread alone,
330	so as to be a witness to the new doctrine of our Lord.
	"All whatsoever You shall give me," he said, "I will tithe a tenth for You,"[40]
	for he took not pleasure in acquiring, but in tithing.
	On this place the righteous Jacob built a house replete with mysteries,
	and with tithes and vows he gave it strong support.

---

[40] Gen. 28:22.

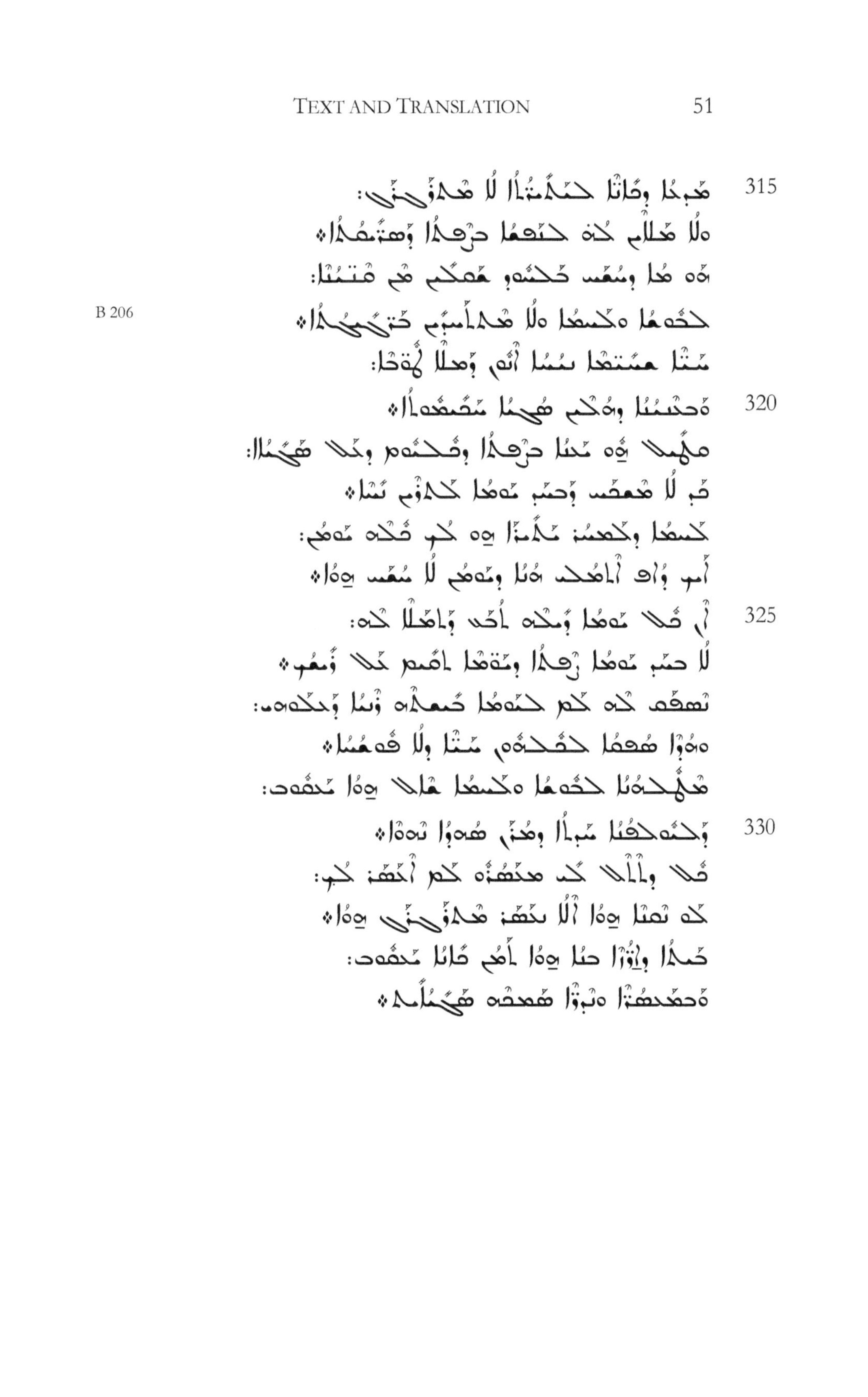

B 206

335 A good will, indeed, urged him to make these offerings;
   Blessed be He who gave him to pay the vows of his discerning choice![41]

End of Homily on Jacob's Revelation at Bethel
composed by Mar Jacob of Serug, Doctor and Bishop of Batnan.

---

[41] Lit., 'of his discernment'.

ܗܘ ܙܒܝܢܐ ܛܒܐ ܚܕ ܗܘܐ ܟܠ ܩܘܪܒܢܐ:
ܒܪܝܟ ܗܘ ܕܚܘܒ ܠܗ ܕܢܦܪܘܩ ܢܕܪܐ ܕܦܘܪܫܘܬܗ܀

ܫܠܡ ܡܐܡܪܐ ܕܥܠ ܚܠܡܗ ܕܝܥܩܘܒ ܕܒܒܝܬ
ܐܝܠ :(ܕܣܝܡ) ܠܡܪܝ ܝܥܩܘܒ ܡܠܦܢܐ: ܐܦܣܩܘܦܐ ܕܒܛܢܢ
ܕܣܪܘܓ.

HOMILY 75: A HOMILY ON OUR LORD AND JACOB, ON THE CHURCH AND RACHEL, AND ON LEAH AND THE SYNAGOGUE

1   The path of the Son was traced out by all the mysteries[42]
       and by their steps they anointed[43] the earth as they journeyed.
       Behold, from the ages He set forth with solemnity to come to the earth,[44]
       and righteous men prepared for Him by their deeds.
5   He set His face so as to come to espouse the Church of the Nations;
       at diverse times He was declared in parables.
       Examine Scripture and there you will find His path,
       for not a single verse[45] is there that does not proclaim Him amidst the readings.
       Take up doctrine as a lamp and enter into the Scriptures,
10   for by it you will be able to behold the beauties of those hidden things.
       In all those books, where is the Son of God not depicted?[46]
       Search to find, if possible, that which cannot be found at all!
       There is not a page whereon the figure of the Son does not rise up,
       nor is there a single text which speaks not plainly of Him.

---

[42] Mysteries (*râzê*): figures, types, symbols.

[43] Or, 'measured'.

[44] See Elkhoury: "The coming down of the Son of God, his betrothal to the Church, and return to his heavenly abode are typologically depicted in the account of Jacob going to Haran, espousing Rachel, the younger daughter of Laban and returning to his Father. In this context, Jacob typifies the Lord Jesus Christ, and Rachel the Church of the Nations. See Elkhoury, *Types and Symbols*, 274–75.

[45] Or, 'stroke'.

[46] Depict (*sûr*).

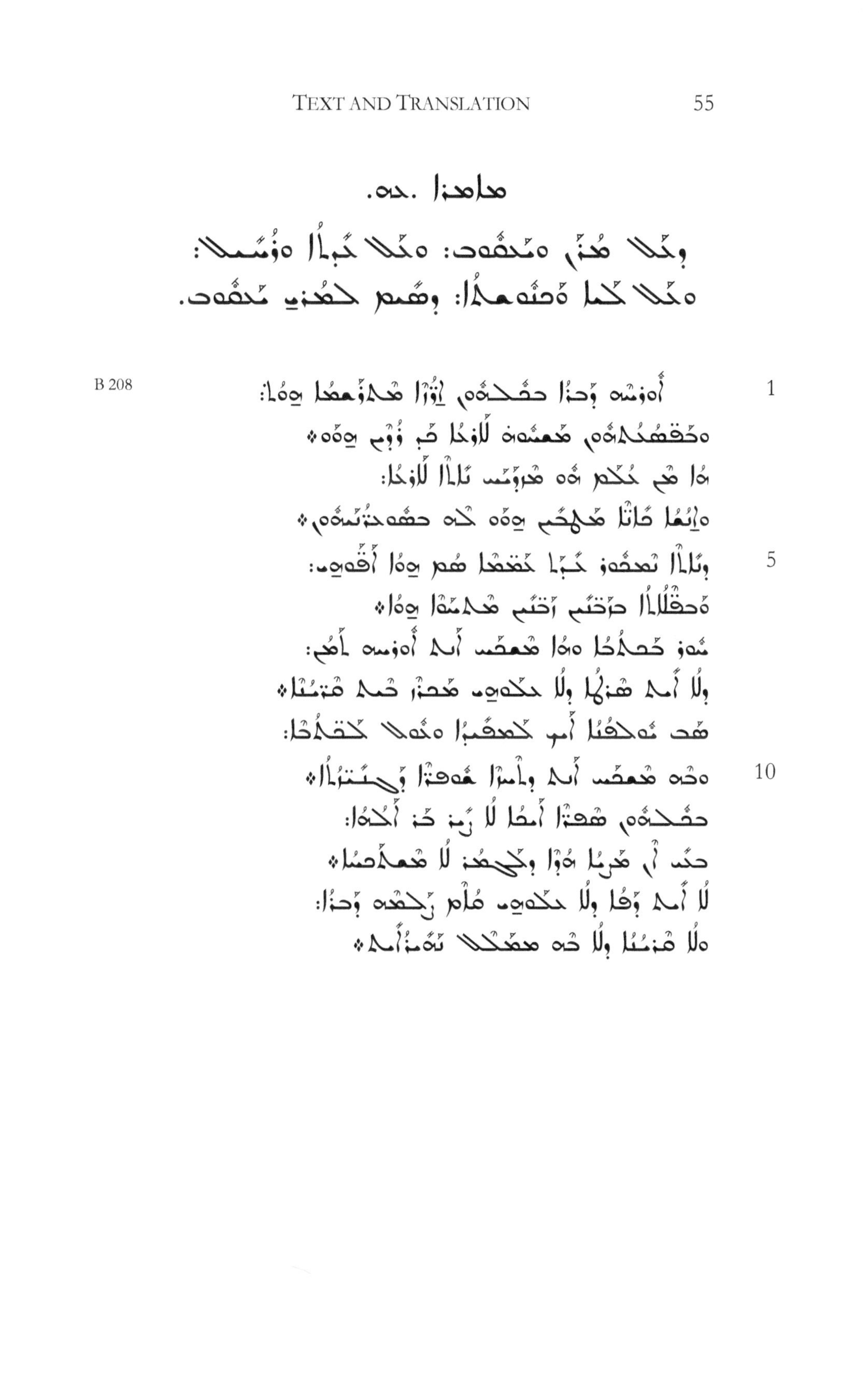

15   Every letter found in the Scriptures is <written> in the Name of the Lord,
and in every utterance He is bountifully interpreted.
At all times it was declared that He will come unto the earth,
even until He came and His heralds had rested from preaching the good tidings.
From the beginning of the world the Mighty One was intent on undertaking His path,[47]
20   and His shadow was visible throughout every generation.
Through the righteous, the kings, the just and the patriarchs,
He confirmed His image, so that the ages might see and await Him.
To the house of Haran, Jacob sent down tidings of His coming,
when he, the righteous prince, was descending to espouse the pagan daughter:
25   she who was brought up among the images of idolatry
to him who was enriched with blessings and revelations.
For the wife who does not believe is sanctified
by the husband who is holy, as Paul writes.[48]
If then Rachel, because of Jacob, was made holy,
30   how much more was the Church of the Nations purified through the Lord of Jacob?
The daughters of the idolater were hallowed through their righteous husband,
showing how the Son sanctified the assemblies of the Nations.
For unless Jacob bore the image of the Son,
he would not have been so famous in his works.

---

[47] Path (*ûrḥâ*).
[48] Cf. 1 Cor. 7:14.

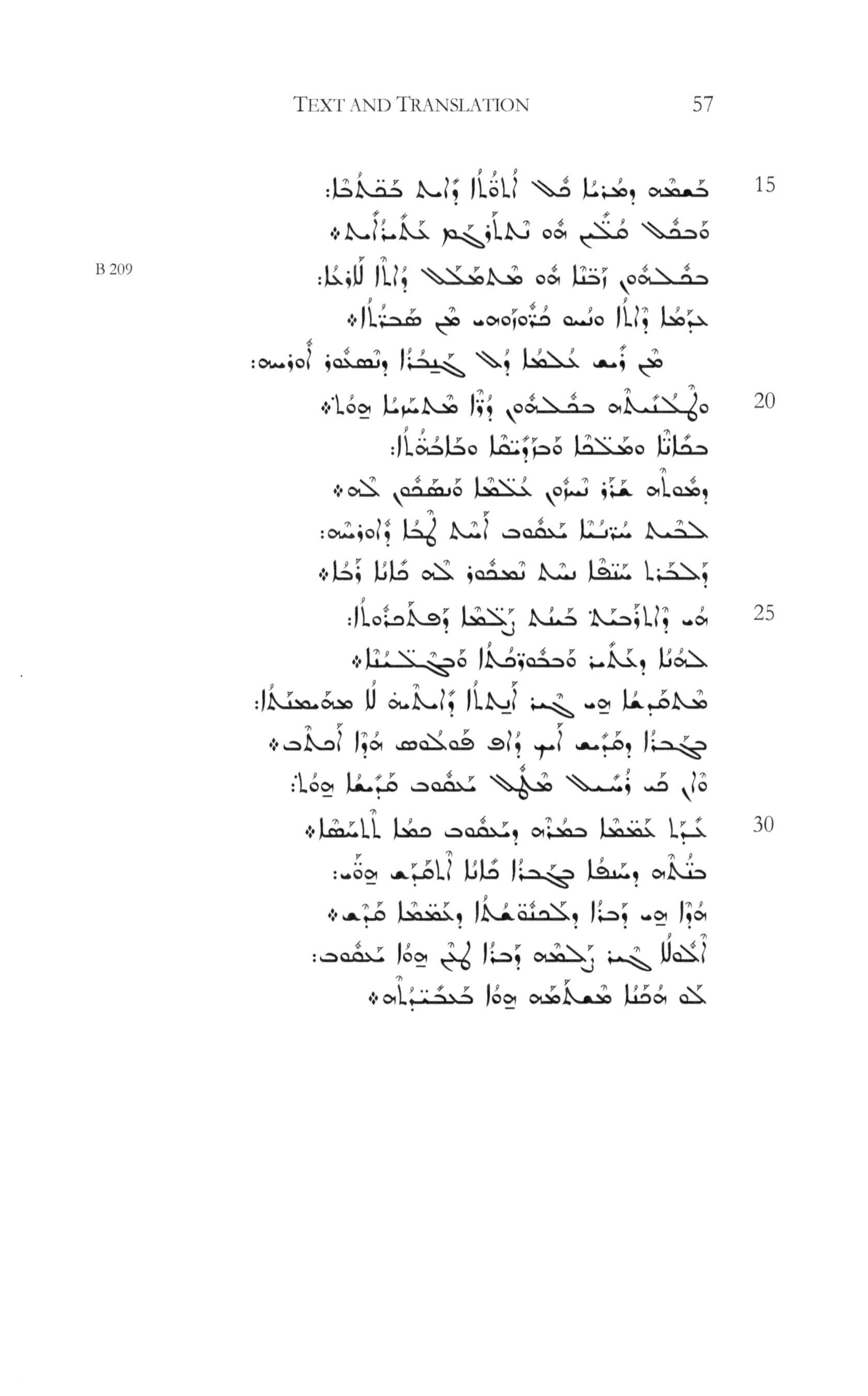

B 209 :

35 How shameful is the tale of Leah, whose eyes were odious!
And for what reason is it narrated, save for the mystery[49] that was brought to pass through her?
How resplendent is her sister Rachel in the readings!
For the beauty of the Church lies hidden in her, and great was the triumph on her account.
How lofty is the tale of Jacob, who was so awesome!
40 For he resembles his Lord, and hence he is exalted in the Scriptures.
Gaze upon his path, which so resembles the path[50] of the Messiah, and understand from this that he walked no path but His.
He was, indeed, a foreshadowing of our Lord in his actions,
for he descended, was betrothed, grew rich and ascended again to his father.
45 Behold how much Jacob, when he journeyed in poverty,
resembled the Son who emptied Himself and came down![51]
Let us, then, relate the things concerning only Jacob's path,
for our Lord's entire path is depicted in it truly.[52]
Jacob set out in poverty to go to Haran,
50 but mysteries accompanied him, so as to minister through him their revelation.[53]
He reached the well, not of water, but of mysteries,
for if you will look, it is more filled with mysteries than with water.
He saw that is was blocked and that there was no bucket to bring up water,[54]
that it was encircled by flocks of sheep and by shepherds.

---

[49] Mystery (*râzâ*).
[50] Path (*ûrḥâ*).
[51] See Phil. 2:7.
[52] See Gen. ch. 29.
[53] Revelation (*gelyânâ*).
[54] Cf. Gen. 29: 1ff.

TEXT AND TRANSLATION

B 210

55	A great stone[55] was found there lying upon the mouth of the well,
	and thirsty sheep gazing at the stone, \<waiting\> for it to be lifted.
	A great weight then lay upon the spring,
	a stone which could scarcely be raised from the well by many men.
	Only the joint strength of many shepherds
60	could push aside the stone of mysteries, only thus it might be lifted.
	Now Jacob arose and beheld the thirsty flocks,
	but he had not the strength to draw back the stone and water them.
	Yet while he stood there, Rachel drew near the flock,
	and as soon as he saw her, he moved the stone aside, that the sheep might drink.[56]
65	Rachel's beauty, when he saw her, incited Jacob
	to roll away the stone that was too heavy for many men.
	The sight of her comeliness served to increase his strength,
	so as to lift the mighty boulder and give the sheep to drink.
	The mystery of the Church lay on her face like a jewel
70	and the righteous man Jacob, her bridegroom, longed greatly for her countenance.
	The assembly of the Nations sprinkled graces upon this daughter of heathen parents,
	so that when Jacob beheld her, he would be aroused to the heroic deed.
	He rolled the great rock from the well and gave the sheep to drink,
	because he saw that the bride of the mysteries[57] was more comely than her companions.

---

[55] Stone (*kêphâ*).

[56] See Gen. 29:10. According to Konat "Jacob acquired the strength to lift the stone – a work usually done by the accumulated strength of many people – only because he served as a type of Christ." See Konat, "Christological Insights," p. 69.

[57] That is, the bride in whom mysteries or types are depicted.

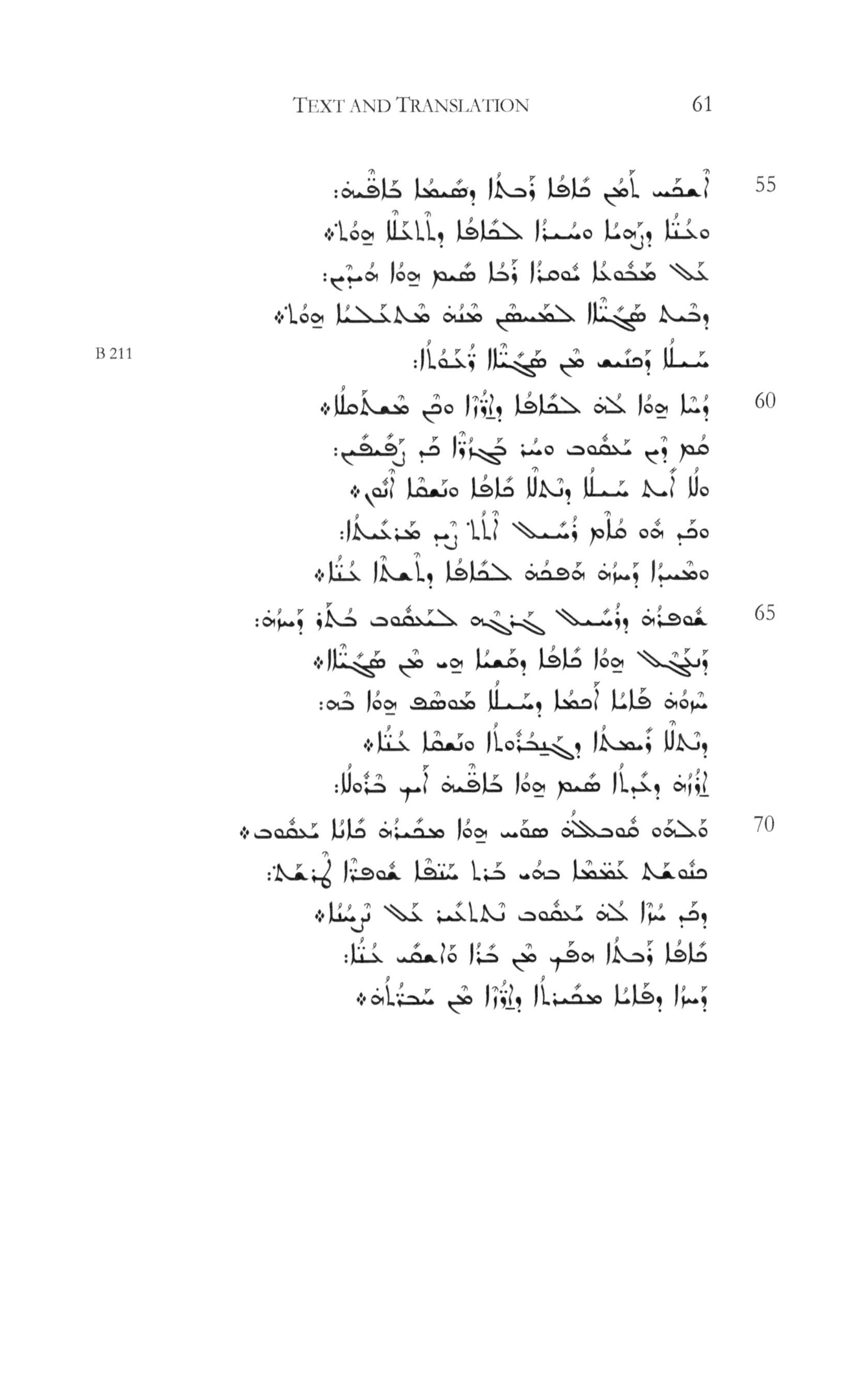

B 211

75 The entire flock drank there because of Rachel,
    who was the cause thereof by her grace, her love and her beauty.
    Think not, my son, that Jacob desired her carnally,
    for even when he kissed her, he wept sorely with great suffering.[58]
    If it were lust, he would not have shed tears in that place,
80 for lust produces gaiety by its fervour.
    Suffering and sorrow are begetters of weeping,
    and wherever there is weeping, there is no lust at all.
    Therefore Jacob was not inflamed by lust,
    but he was afflicted by the suffering of the mysteries of the Son.
85 Who has kissed his bride with weeping, save Jacob?
    For he beheld the mystery of the Church in Rachel as she was betrothed <to him>.
    And it was also fitting that he wept and suffered when he embraced her,
    so as to signify in his betrothal the sufferings of the Son.
    By his tears[59] he portrayed an image of the Passion of the Son of God,
90 for when He betrothed the Church, He suffered, and only then was she betrothed.
    Behold, how much greater is the path of the Son than that of His heralds,
    and the marriage of the Royal Bridegroom than that of His envoys.
    Jacob shed tears for Rachel when he espoused her,
    and our Lord sprinkled the Church with His tears when He redeemed her.

---

[58] See Gen. 29:11.
[59] Tears (*dem 'ê*).

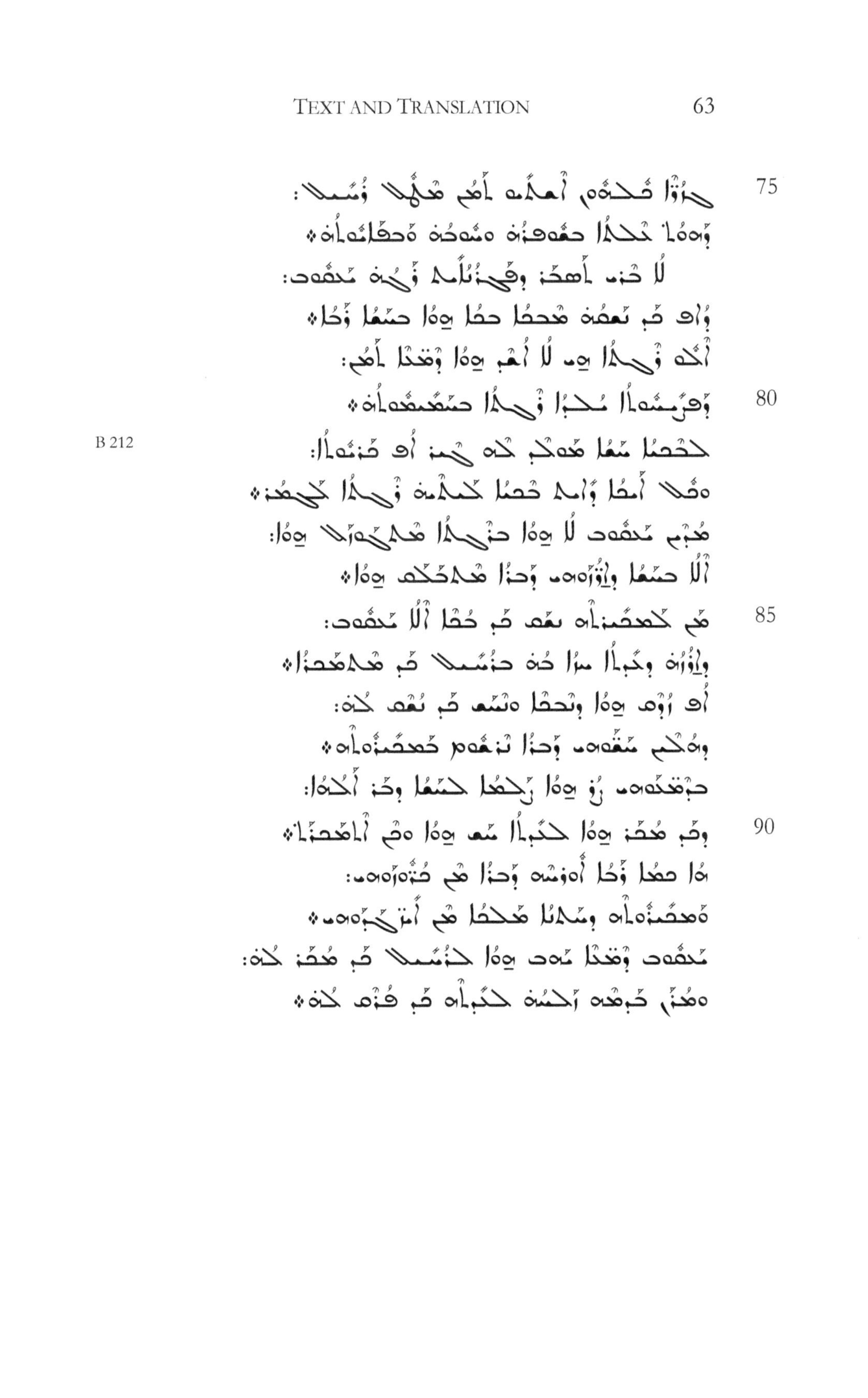

95   So His tears were a foreshadowing of <our Lord's> blood,
for unless it is through suffering, tears do not flow from the pupils.
Therefore the mourning of the righteous Jacob was a shadow
    of that great Passion whereby the Church of the Nations was redeemed.
Come, see our Lord, who has come to the world from the Father,
100   emptying Himself so as to accomplish His path in a humble manner!
He beheld sin lying upon the wellspring of the world,
and that there was no draught of life to give mankind refreshment.
He beheld the Nations, like flocks, in great thirst
    and that the fount of life was blocked up by sin as though by a stone.
105   He looked upon the Church as on Rachel, and longed to meet her;
and like that stone, He rolled away the heavy weight of sin.
He opened up the baptismal font for His betrothed, that she might bathe there,
    and He drew and let the Nations of the earth drink like those flocks.
He lifted up the weight of sin by His mighty strength,
110   and He revealed a spring that gave a sweet draught to all the world.
He poured out a drink for all the Nations because of the Church,
even as all the flocks drank because of Rachel.
Now unless this mystery had descended upon Jacob,
    a mere person, he would not have been able to remove that great stone.

TEXT AND TRANSLATION

B 213

115	The one who wishes only by sight to accept these things,
	let him go and see that stone which is too heavy even for mighty persons!
	Scarcely could a group of people turn and roll that stone;
	could one person alone, then, move it however little?
	Unless the mystery had taken hold of his hand there,
120	Jacob could not have budged that stone, being a man of little stature.
	But since the shadow of the Great Shepherd rested upon him,
	his strength surpassed that of all the shepherds.
	He drew water and gave Rachel's sheep to drink as in a mystery,
	and when Laban heard of Jacob's deed, he rejoiced to meet him.
125	Wholeheartedly did the idolater receive the righteous man,
	and he began to make a covenant with him concerning service.
	"Let it be known," said Laban, "what your reward will be,
	for it is not right that you should serve for nothing, if you are my kinsman."[60]
	And Jacob said, "For Rachel shall I serve you;[61]
130	give me your younger daughter as a wife and this will be a good reward.
	Seven years I shall work with you for Rachel,
	and you shall give me nothing but her.
	This is the wage which I ask you to render me:
	Rachel, your daughter, when I have served you diligently."

---

[60] Cf. Gen. 29:15.
[61] Cf. Gen. 29:18.

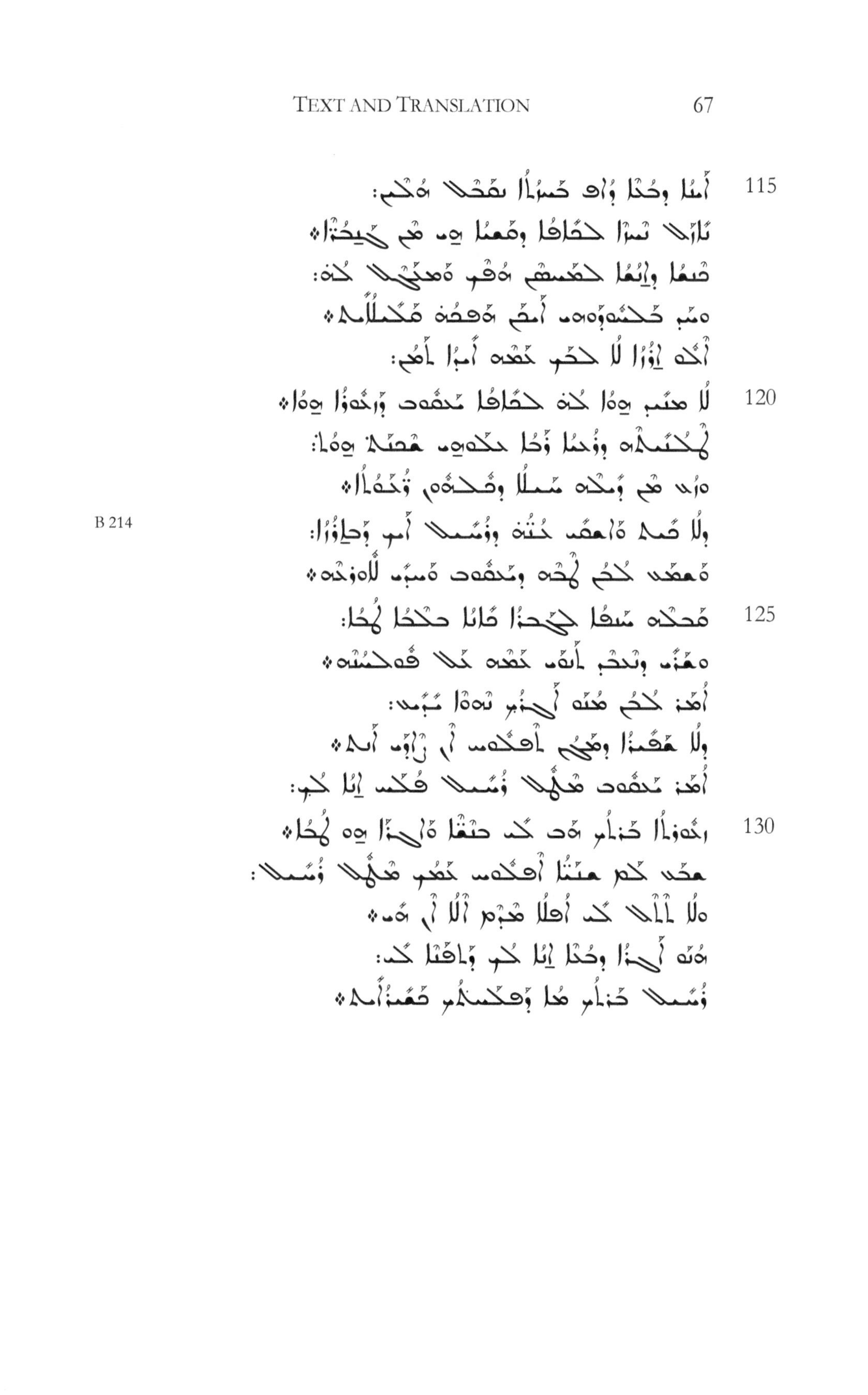

135   Here the entire type of our Lord is enacted,
        for on account of the Church He gave Himself over to great toil.
        The Son of God invested His sufferings because of His love,
        so that by His wounds He would betroth the Church that was abandoned.
        Because of the worship of the idols, He suffered on the Cross,
140   so that after His toils she might become His in a sanctified manner.
        He accepted to shepherd all the flocks of mankind
        with the great staff of the Crucifixion, when He suffered.
        Peoples, worlds, classes, assemblies, and localities
        He accepted to shepherd, and in return He received the Church alone.
145   With labour and weariness and by wounds He tended the flock:
        when He underwent sufferings and stripes on its account;
        when He stumbled so as to gather \<the sheep\> that were perishing,
        and bent down His shoulder to carry those who were gone astray;
        when He stood amidst the multitudes in behalf of the flock,
150   and instead of thorns, was pierced with nails for its sake.
        As He bore these things, there was no cool water, but only stripes.
        And for the scorching heat He received the point of spear in the flock's behalf.
        When Satan and death, those wolves, menaced Him,
        He being crucified withstood the suffering and did not yield.
155   So Jacob made a covenant with Laban for Rachel,
        that he would tend the sheep and take to wife her whom he requested.
        He served Laban seven years for his daughter,
        but his long toil was mitigated by his great love.
        The years and months of his service were short to him,

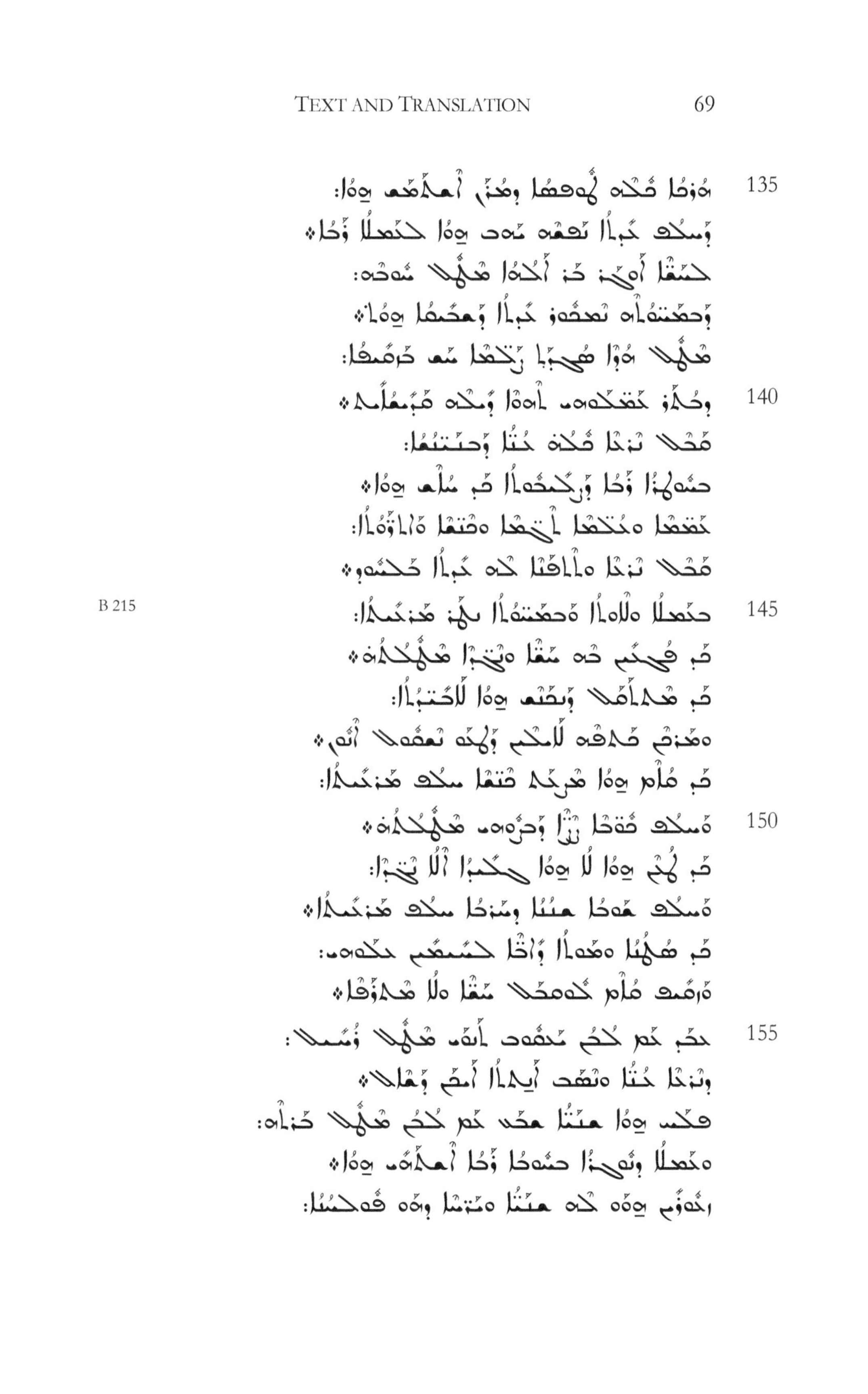

160 because the reward set for him was so great in his eyes.
The beauty of Rachel stood before him like a silver coin,
and stirred him not to lose heart over when he would receive her.
He reckoned the years he toiled as fleeting days
because of the covenant that he cherished from the beginning.
165 He was able to abate the chill of night by his love,
and likewise the heat of day by the cherished reward that was set for him.
At last the time was fulfilled when the shepherd should receive his reward,
but the treacherous Laban schemed to cheat him.
The wedding feast was held so that the bridegroom might rejoice in his betrothed,
170 but instead of Rachel, Leah went in because of her father's guile.
She, whose eyes were unlovely, was carefully instructed to veil herself,
until the righteous bridegroom be ensnared by her; then she be recognized.
Laban secretly plotted with her before she entered,
and taught her words to say if she were called by name.
175 As she disguised her scheme, she was thought to be chaste;
she hid her uncomely appearance and Jacob believed it to be modesty.
They concealed Rachel so that the deceit regarding her should not be detected,
lest she whom they veiled be shown to be Leah.
Leah was veiled and her sister was hid among the handmaids,
180 and who but Laban recognized a secret in this?
Rachel was passed over and in a veil Leah stood forth;
Laban beguiled the righteous Jacob concerning his betrothed.
The fair one was passed over and she entered whose appearance was odious;
for here too, hidden mysteries occurred.

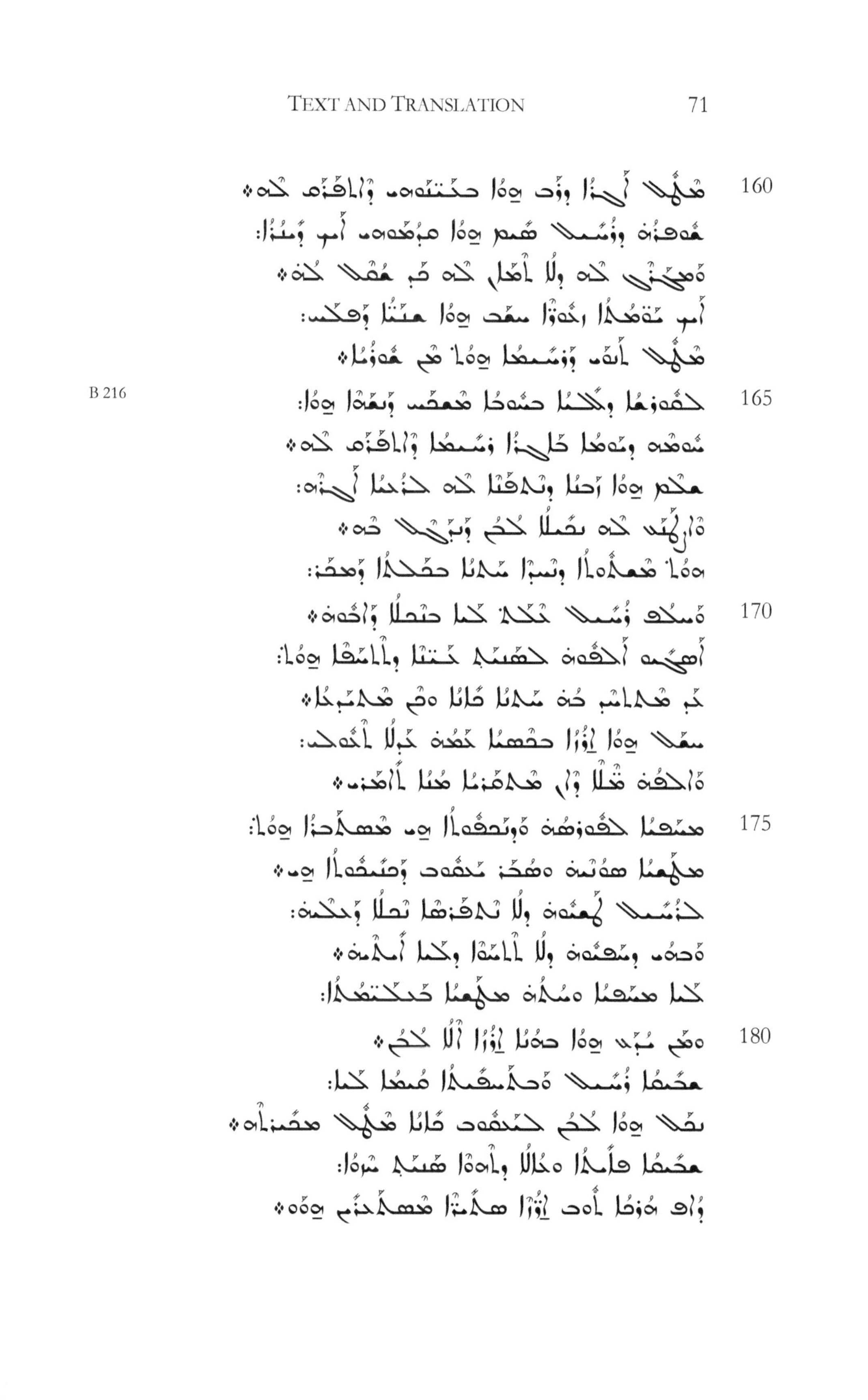

185 The bride deceived the bridegroom and he erred, for she was not Rachel;
and he was captured by her, not perceiving the plot against him.
Instead of the fair, the ill-favored one entered guilefully,
for she would not have gone in unless she was considered to be Rachel.
Dawn came and Laban's deceit was unmasked to Jacob,
190 and the uncomely visage that was concealed became visible.
By night and by Leah, Jacob was led astray as in a dream,
but when the morning dawned, the abhorrent deed became plain to him.
Evening had veiled the bride and had given her cunningly,
but early dawn revealed her, causing the bridegroom to see her and despise her.
195 She who was rejected was given to the man under a name that was not her own,
for her own name, even as her appearance, could not be used.
She who entered was concealed by Rachel's name, she not being Rachel,
so that by the beauty of the one, the guileful Laban could give the twain.
He placed Rachel's beauty upon Leah, and bringing her forth he gave her,
200 for unless Rachel stayed behind, the other could not have come forward, because of her appearance.
Laban craftily placed the name of the comely upon the homely,
so that with the beauty of the one the two brides might be adorned.
But morning came and the bridegroom beheld his bride and was astonished,[62]
for she that had been given him to rejoice with was not for whom he had asked.

---

[62] See Gen. 29:25.

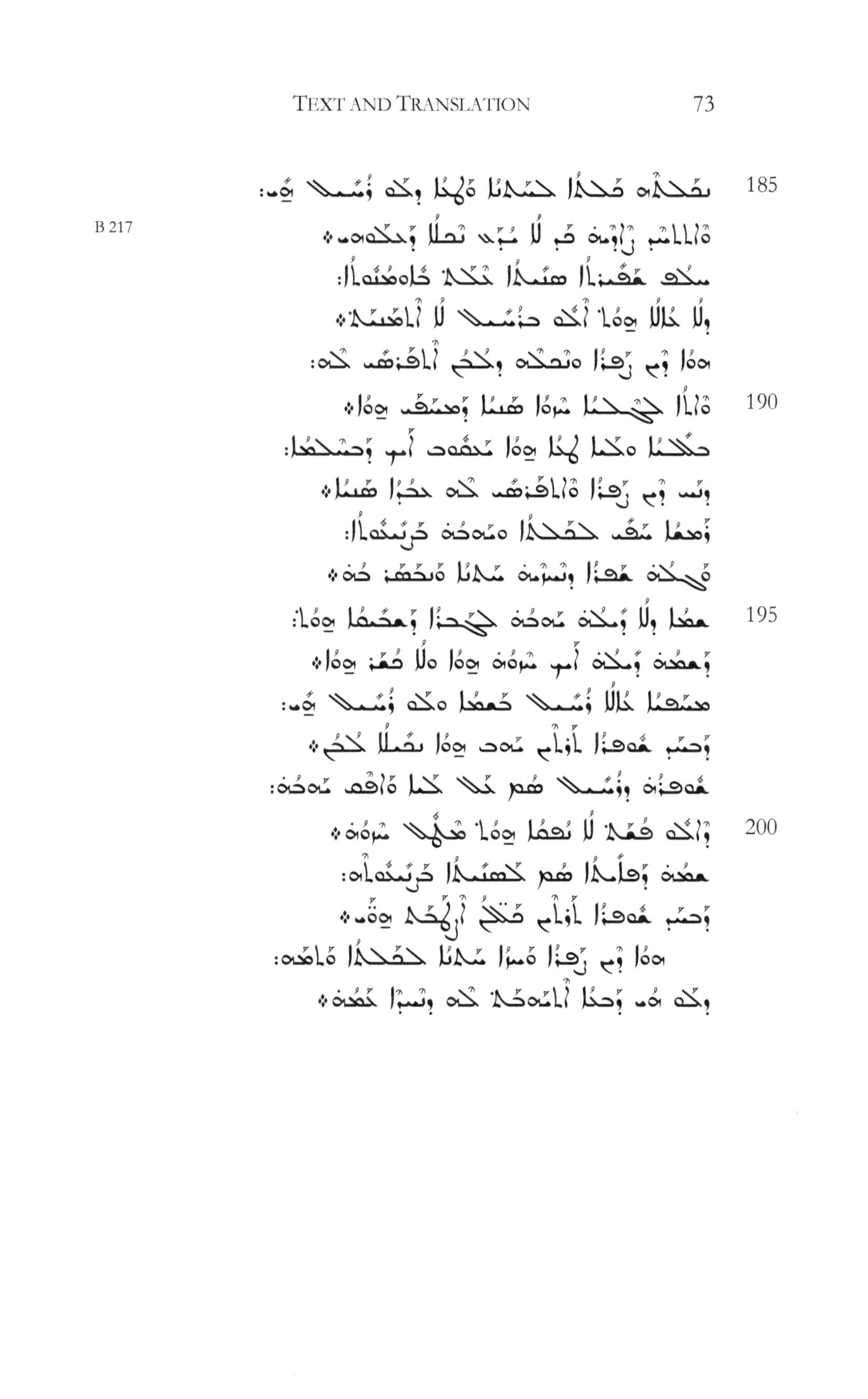

B 217

205 He served diligently with the flocks for the fair one,
    but when the wedding feast arrived, the odious one came forth for the rejoicing.
    Then the righteous man began to reproach the pagan for his slyness:
    "What is this that you have done to me , after all my labors?
    I served for Rachel; why, then, have you given me Leah?
210 I betrothed the fair one; why was the one given me whose appearance is odious?
    Why have you deceived me, changing my wages after my service ?
    You have annulled the covenant that we made in the beginning.
    Where is Rachel for whose sake I served you?
    Leah, whom I did not ask for, came to me and I knew it not."
215 Then Laban said, "It is a custom in all our land
    that the younger is not given before the elder.
    But I will not hinder you from taking Rachel also, if you wish:
    Take the two, since our law is not to be changed."
    Here Laban's stratagem employed craftiness,
220 it seized as a pretext that which was the custom of the land.
    Jacob agreed to take the twain from Laban's household,
    although he desired only one, she who was beautiful.
    Here the mystery of the <two> assemblies was enacted:
    in the two sisters who were given to the one man.
225 Jacob depicts[63] the entire path[64] of the Son of God,
    and without His types[65] he could not take a single step.
    Even though Laban devised treachery against the righteous man,
    providence[66] wrought its own <work> in that wedding banquet.
    Even though Jacob was exceedingly grieved[67] by what came to pass,

---

[63] Depicts (*ṣûr*).
[64] Path (*ûrḥâ*).
[65] Types (*ṭûpsê*).
[66] Providence (*mdabbrânûṯâ*).
[67] Or, 'disgusted,' 'indignant.'

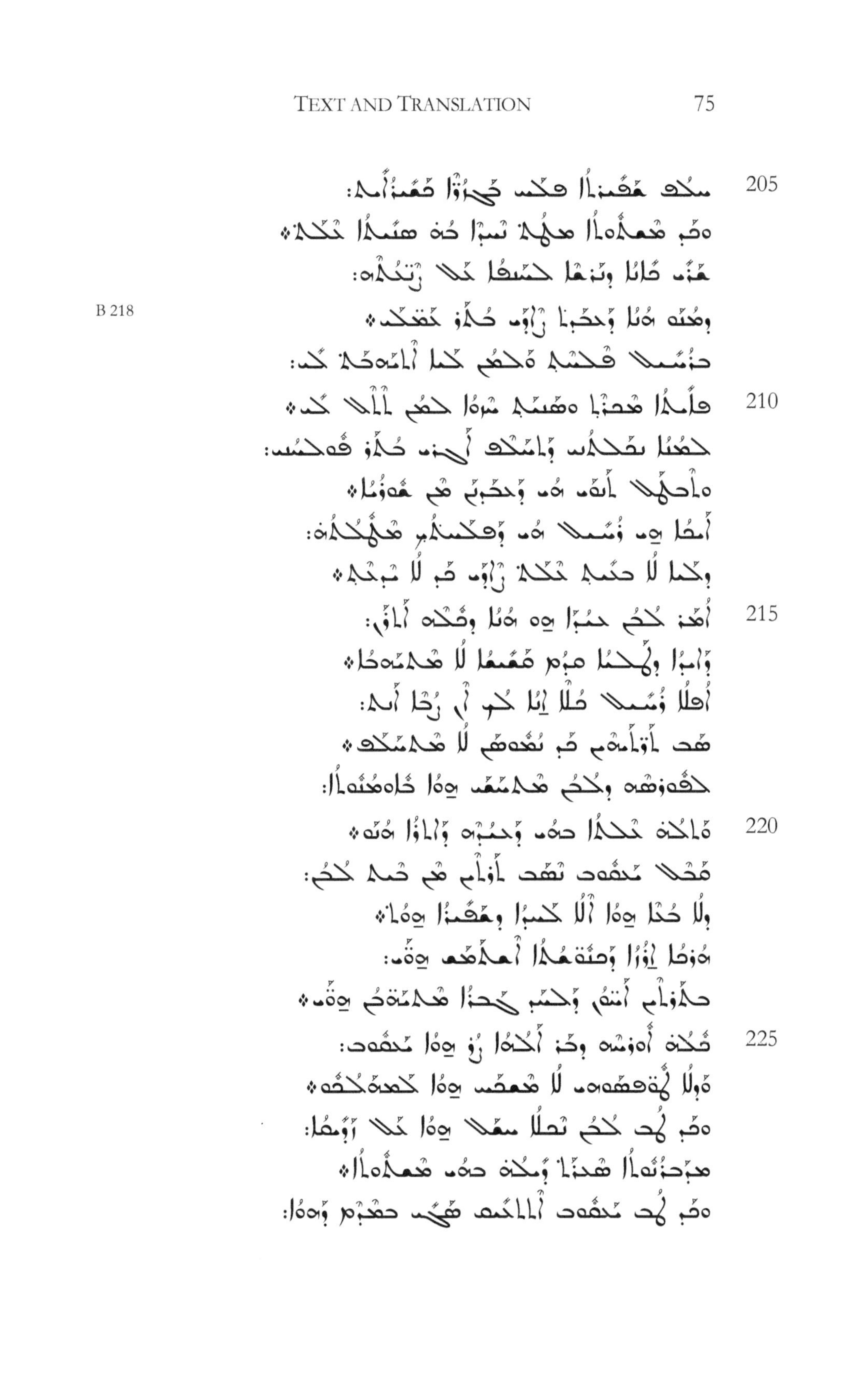

230   a great mystery shone forth in the sisters who were given.
A shadow of a great body[68] was that deed,
and unless it were thus, it could not have come to pass.
That beautiful thing which was done was not Jacob's doing,
nor was it Laban who invented that great discovery.
235   Together with the righteous man the mystery entered the pagan's house,
and it betrothed the two sisters so that it might manifest itself clearly.
The Nation and the Nations were signified by Leah and Rachel;
the Synagogue and the Church were heralded in the two sisters.
God has called all Nations into communion with Himself,
240   for there is not one Nation on the earth that is not His own.
The calling of the Nations was a thing beloved of the Creator,
even that all should come and become His through repentance.[69]
He loved the Church and sought that she might become His,
for that Bride is even more beautiful than Rachel.
245   When the daughter of the Nations was betrothed by God,
the Synagogue of the Nation went before her and came to Adonai.
With the veil that Moses stretched over his face,[70]
and also with Leah's covering, fashioned because she was the elder,
the daughter of the Hebrews hid herself and stood before Adonai,

---

[68] Or, 'a great matter'. Or again, 'the Great Body', meaning the Church, the Lord's Body.

[69] Repentance (*tyâbûtâ*): in Jewish midrashic material, some beautiful passages can be found on repentance. It is considered to be one of the seven things created before the creation of the world, "The power of Repentance" in Pirke Rabbi Eliezer, 337–44. (PRE is a 9th cent. redaction, most of the material belonging to an earlier period). See also Urbach, *The Sages*, 462–71. Scholem quotes a Babylonian Gaon (8th cent.) linking the path of repentance with the "ecstatic progress through the seven heavens leading to the throne of glory," *Major Trends*, 78.

[70] See Ex. 34:33–35. See also Mar Jacob, "On the Veil of Moses," S. Brock (tr).

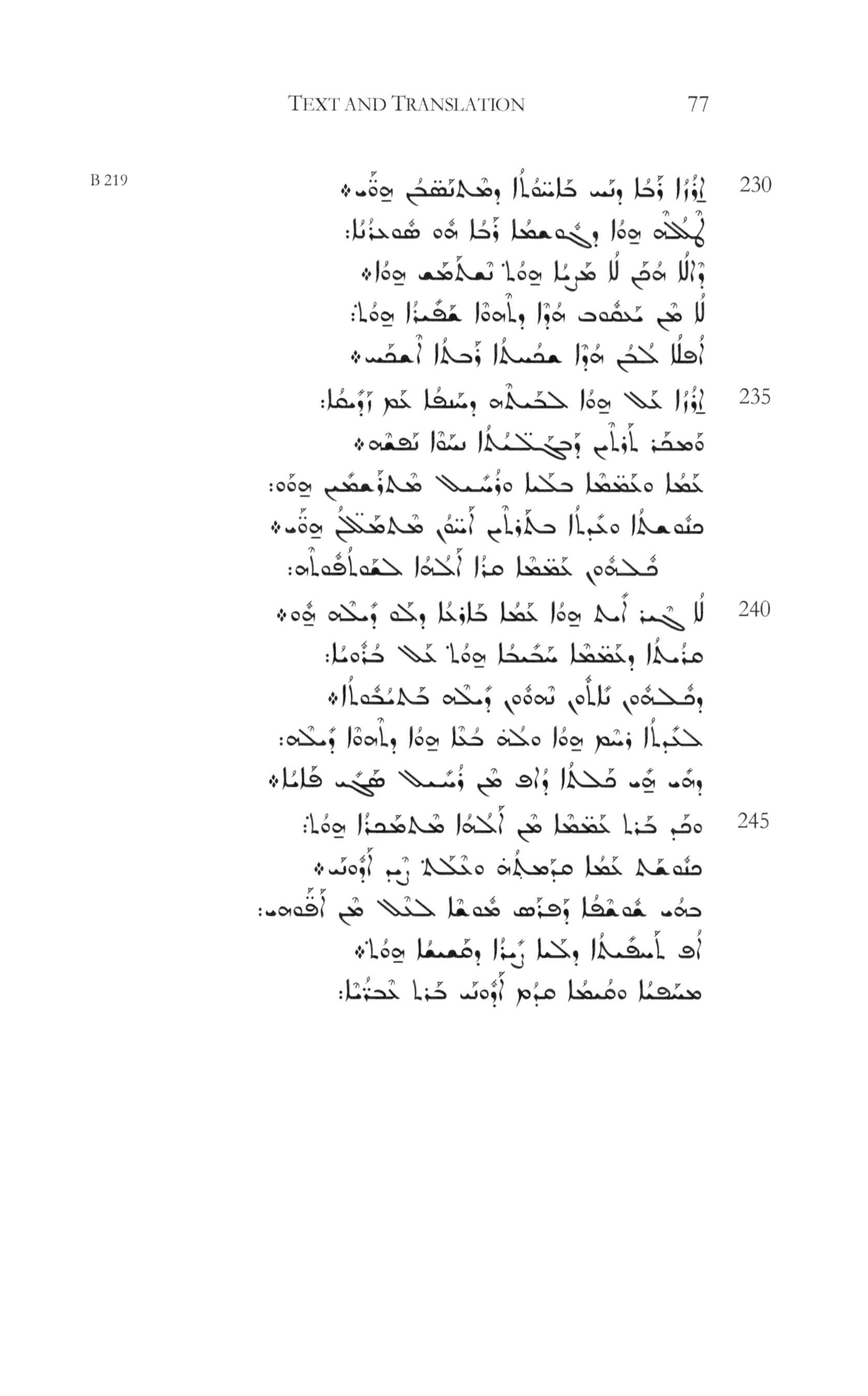

B 219

250	concealing her vileness by Moses' radiance, and she was not known.
	Being proclaimed by the viewers to be the great Church,
	she sought for a covering, that she might not be detected.
	Her appearance was odious, even more than Leah's, the daughter of the Haranites;
	her light was taken away, for her eyes were not even soft.[71]
255	She gazed upon the calf and called it 'Lord'[72] because she was blind,
	for she had not the sight to distinguish the truth.
	She, then, who was bereft of light, entered in first,
	while the Church, whose beauty resembled Rachel's, was left aside.
	She[73] was veiled by Moses[74] and no man knew that she was blind;
260	and in her covering she appeared to be beautiful.
	She who was rich in comeliness was hidden among the Nations and unknown.
	While she who was entirely odious was concealed and entered the house of God.
	On account of the Church, God served mankind
	through revelations[75] and through wondrous deeds.
265	And because the daughter of the Nation was the elder, though she was odious,
	she was given to the Lord, like Leah, the elder.
	For this Nation was, indeed, God's first-born,
	and though the daughter of the Nations was beautiful, she was left aside.
	It was not seemly that the younger should go in before the elder,

---

[71] Gen. 29:17; The LXX reads 'weak', 'infirm'.
[72] See Ex.32:8,9.
[73] I.e., the Synagogue.
[74] Or, 'she veiled herself in Moses'.
[75] Revelations (*gelyânê*).

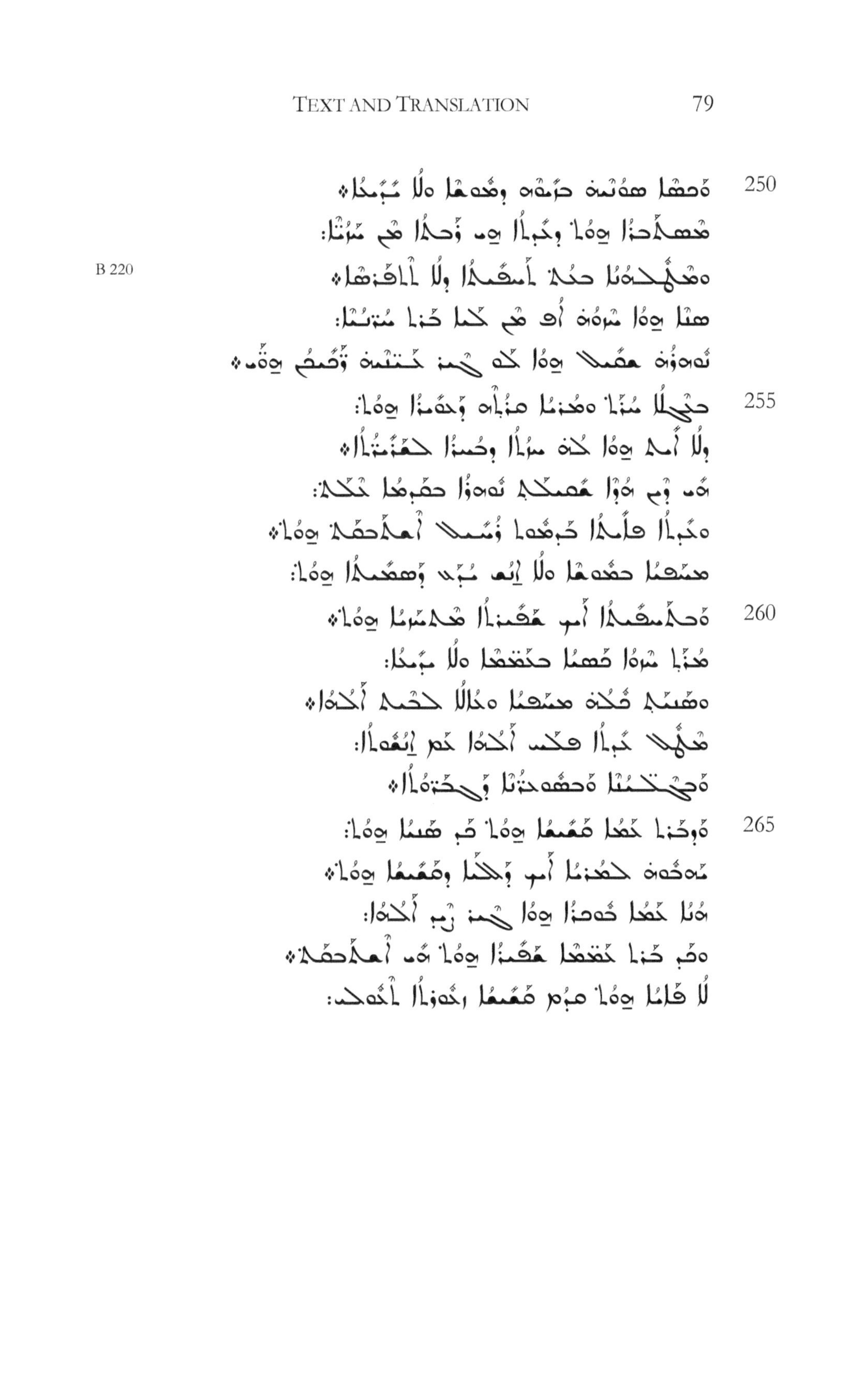

270   and so Laban bore witness that instead of Rachel, he gave Leah.
In the middle of the night, Moses led her out of Egypt,
so that no one might know how odious the bride was that he brought forth.
She came in the night even as Leah also entered in the night,
but the morning unmasked both, that they were odious.

275   Rachel the younger, and the Church, the youthful Maiden, were beautiful,
and at last they entered in, because the light made manifest their beauty.
Jacob betrothed the pleasing beauty, whose appearance was comely,
whose visage was lovely, whose countenance was desirable, who was entirely glorious.
But he was given her whose eyes were odious, whose light was feeble,

280   who was wearisome of appearance, sullen of countenance and covered with blemishes.
And our Lord, likewise, betrothed the great Church, the daughter of kings,
who knew the Father, who worshipped the Son, who received the Spirit.
Yet there was given Him the Synagogue of the Nation that worshipped idols,
who forged the calf, who rejected the Father, and crucified the Son.

285   The bridegrooms loved the younger because they were beautiful,
even the Church and Rachel, who without guile loved their spouses.
Not with guile did Rachel go to the righteous one,
nor with a covering does the Church stand before the Holy One.
Revealed was the face of the Church, adorned with beauty greater than Rachel's;

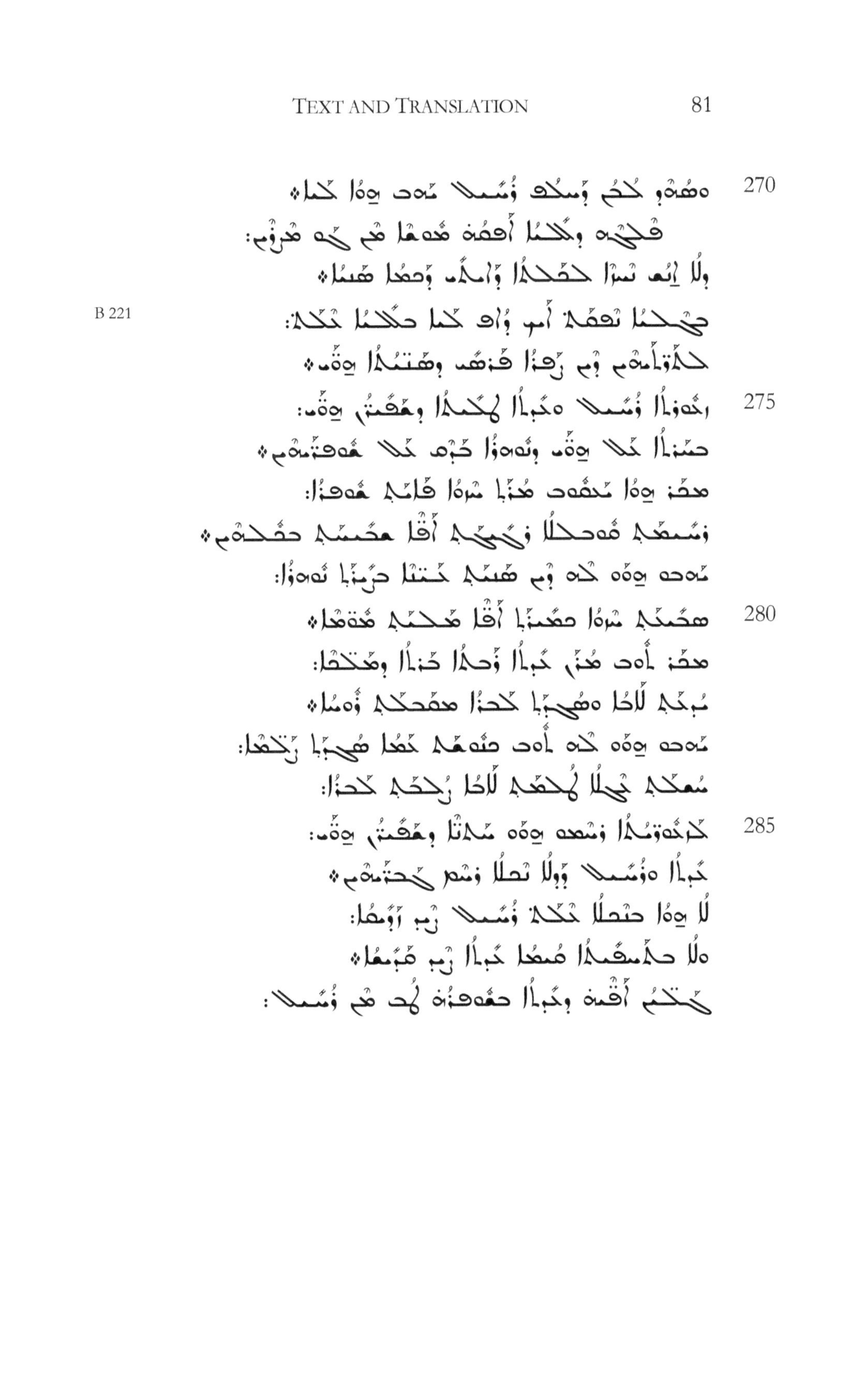

 B 221

290 in the morning she entered, so that all could behold her beauty.
The Synagogue and Leah could not have entered without a veil,
for they had no beauty for which they might be loved.
Devices, deceits, and cunning did they employ
with God, as also with Jacob who bore His likeness
295 But since artifice cannot stand before the truth;
the dawn, even the Cross, unmasked their guileful deeds.
In the morning Jacob beheld Leah, that she was odious.
And the dawning of the Son revealed the Synagogue, that she was double-minded.
The Church's face was revealed and she stood before the truth,
300 and was not veiled, for her beauty proclaimed her triumph.
Her appearance spoke in place of beautiful adornments,
and she entered not with another's likeness, hiding her blemishes.
There is no blemish in her beauty which might be hid;
she resembles Rachel "who was beautiful of appearance and fair of face."[76]
305 These mysteries came to pass in the house of Laban,
for the Son's entire path was signified in Jacob.
He betrothed Rachel but Leah entered, as it is recorded;
instead of the daughter of the Nations, the Synagogue entered though she was odious.
In her whose eyes were soft he beheld the Synagogue symbolically,
310 for the latter was more odious than Leah by her very deeds.
"This people's heart," it is said, "has waxed gross, and their ears are dull of hearing,
and their eyes they have closed, lest they should hear and lest they should see."[77]
The eyes, indeed, of that <odious one>[78] were not soft,
but she blocked her eyes and her ears from understanding.

---

[76] Gen. 29:17.

[77] Matt. 13:15.

[78] There is a two-syllable lacuna in the Syriac, which *sanya*, "hateful, odious," would fit.

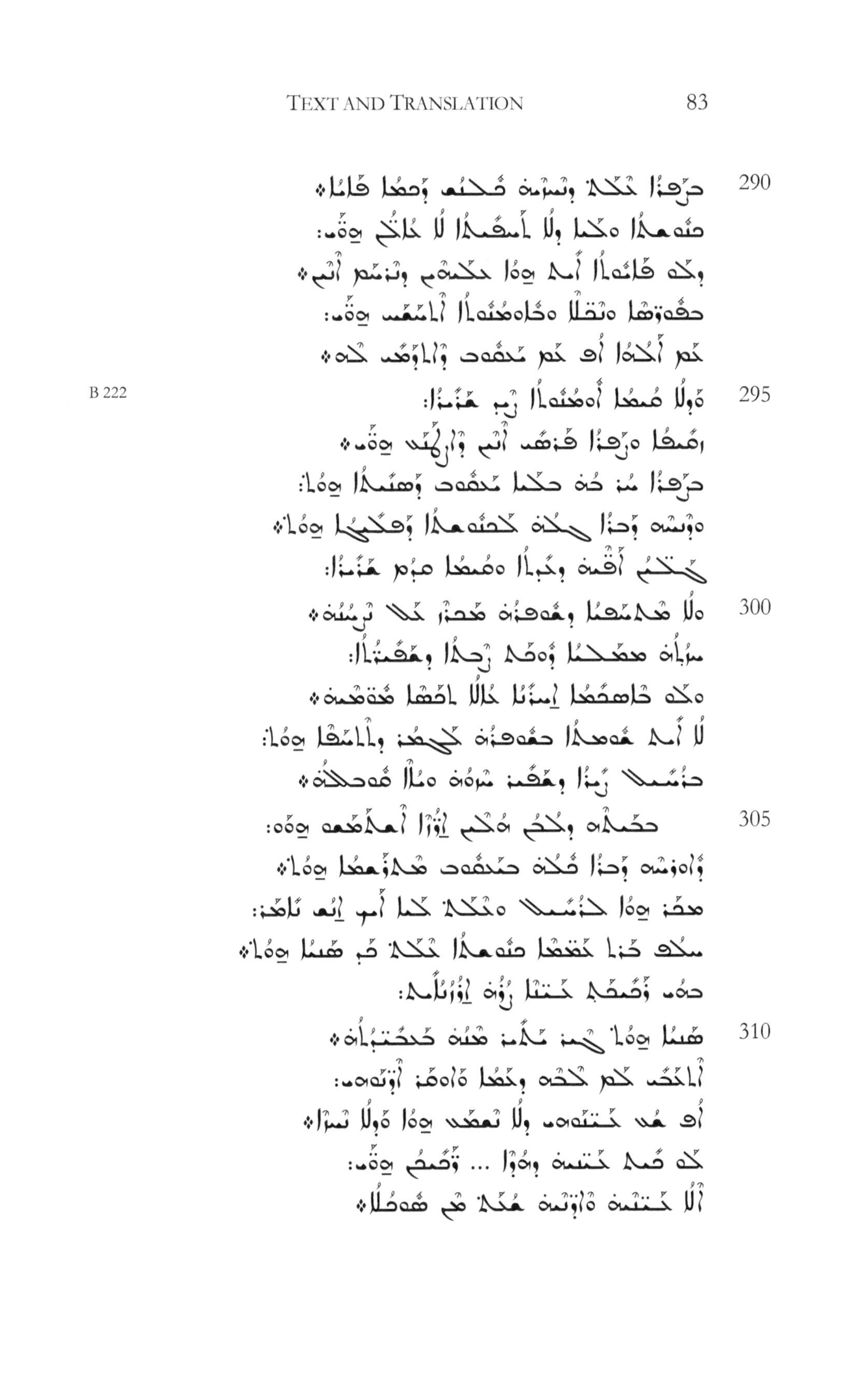

315   Leah was not blameworthy because her eyes were odious and wretched,
for against her will she was repugnant, as it were in a mystery.
But the Synagogue is blameworthy because voluntarily she shut her eyes.
for very odious is the blemish that comes from free will.
Grace be upon Leah who loved her husband though she was despised![79]
320   Woe to the Synagogue who was odious and hated Him that loved her!
She stopped up her eyes and ears, that daughter of the Hebrews;
how much more odious was she than Leah, the daughter of the Haranites!
The Church, though rejected, was loved by reason of her beauty,
thus resembling Rachel who was put aside, though she was fair.
325   Jacob took the odious one as well as the one adorned with beauty,
thus resembling our Lord who betrothed the Nation and the Nations to His Gospel.
These mysteries by these just persons were traced out clearly,
and for this reason their excellence shone brightly in every place.
By Jacob and by Laban's daughter were our Lord and the Church represented.
330   Blessed be He by whose mysteries the righteous shone forth gloriously in their deeds!

The End

---

[79] See Gen. 29:31.

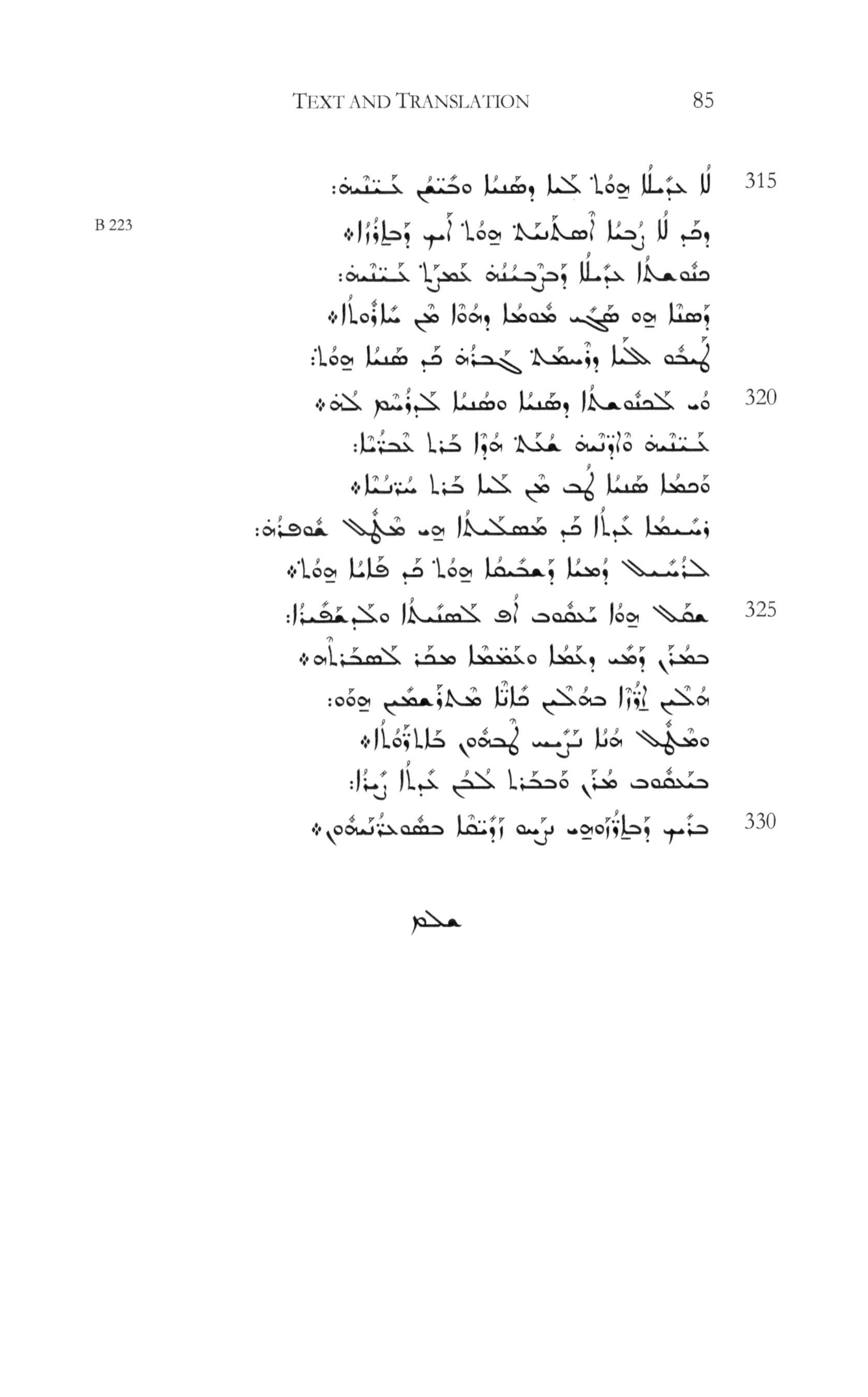

B 223

BIBLIOGRAPHY OF WORKS CITED

M. Albert (tr.), *Jacques de Saroug. Homélies contre les Juifs*, PO 38 (Brepols, 1976).

___ *Les Lettres de Jacques de Saroug, Patrimoine Syriaque* 3 (Kaslik, 2004).

___ "Mimro de Jacques de Saroug sur la Synagogue et l'Église," *OS* 7 (1962), 143–62.

H. Alfeyev, *The Spiritual World of Isaac the Syrian* (Kalamazoo MI, 2000).

S. Beggiani, *Early Syriac Theology* (Washington, D.C. : Catholic University of America Press, 2014).

___"The Typological Approach of Syriac Sacramental Theology," *TS* 64 (2003): 543–57.

B.M. Boulos Sony, "La Methode Exégètique de Jacques de Saroug," *PdO* 9 ('79–'80): 67–103.

T. Bou Mansour, *La Théologie de Jacques de Saroug* Vol I (Lebanon, 1993).

S. Brock, "Baptismal Themes in the Writings of Jacob of Serugh," *OCA* 205 (1978): 325–47.

___ "The Bridal Chamber of the Light: A Distinctive Feature of the Syriac Liturgical Tradition," *Harp* 18 (2005): 179–91.

___ *Bride of Light,* Môrân 'Eth'ô 6 (Kerala, 2nd ed. 2009).

___ *Jacob of Serug's Homily on the Veil on Moses' Face*, (tr.) TeCLA 20 (Gorgias Press, 2009).

___ "Jacob of Serug's verse homily on Tamar," *LM* 115 (2002): 279–315.

___ *The Luminous Eye*, Cistercian Publications (Kalamazoo MI, 1992).

___ "The Mysteries Hidden in the Side of Christ," *Sob/ECR* 7:6 (1978): 462–72.

___ "The Wedding Feast of Blood on Golgotha. An unusual aspect of John 19:34 in Syriac tradition," *Harp* 6.2 (1993): 121–34.

R. Chesnut, *Three Monophysite Christologies: Severus of Antioch, Philoxenus of Mabbug and Jacob of Serug* (Oxford, 1976).

A. Elkhoury, "Jesus Christ, the Eye of Prophecy," in *Les Exégètes Syriaques: Actes du Colloque* XIII, *Patrimoine Syriaque*, ed. Paul Feghali (Lebanon: CERO, 2015): 1–27.

___ *Types and Symbols of the Church in the Writings of Jacob of Sarug* (Bavaria, diss., 2017).

P.M. Forness, "Cultural Exchange and Scholarship on Eastern Christianity. An Early Modern Debate over Jacob of Serugh's Christology," *JEasternCS* 70 (2018): 257–84.

___ *Preaching Christology in the Roman Near East: a Study of Jacob of Serugh* (Oxford University Press, 2018).

G. Friedlander (tr.), *Pirke de Rabbi Eliezer. The Chapters of Rabbi Eliezer the Great* (New York: Sepher-Hermon Press, 1981, 4th ed.).

A. Golitzin, "The Image and Glory of God in Jacob of Serug's Homily, *On the Chariot that Ezekiel the Prophet Saw*," *SVTQ* 47 (2003): 323–64.

F. Graffin (tr.), "Mimro de Jacques de Sarug sur la Vision de Jacob a Bethel," *OS* 5 (1960): 225–46.

___ "The Theme of Church as Bride in the Syriac Liturgies and Patristic Literature," *Liturgy* 24 (1990): 78–101.

S.H. Griffith, "The Image of the Image Maker in the Poetry of St. Ephraem the Syrian," *StPatr* 25 (1993): 258–69.

M. Hansbury, "*Insight Without Sight*: Wonder as an Aspect of Revelation in the Discourses of Isaac the Syrian," *JCSSS* 8 (2008): 60–73.

___ "Love as an Exegetical Principle in Jacob of Serug," *Harp* XXVII (2011): 353–68.

A. Harrak (tr.), "Memra 33 of Narsai: The Sacramental Nature of the 'Church of the Nations'," *PdO* 41 (2015): 181–203.

S. Harvey, "Bride of Blood, Bride of Light: Biblical Women as images of Church in Jacob of Serug," in *Malphono W-Rabo D-Malphone: Studies in Honor of Sebastian P. Brock*, ed. George A. Kiraz (Gorgias Press, 2008): 177–204.

___ and Ophir Münz-Manor, *Jacob of Serug's Homily on Jephthah's Daughter* (Piscataway, 2010).

T. Jansma, "The Credo of Jacob of Serugh," *NAKG* 44 (1960): 18–36.

S. Johnson, "The Sinful Woman: a memra by Jacob of Serug," *Sob/ECR* 24 (2002): 56–88.

S.K. Joshua, *Church as the Bride of Christ, a Unique Divine-Human Relationship Model: A Study Based on the Select Homilies of Mar Jacob of Serug (451–521)*, (Bangalore diss., 2015).

Cyril Aphrem Karim, *Symbols of the Cross in the Writings of the Early Syriac Fathers* (Gorgias Press, 2004).

G.A. Kiraz (ed.) *Jacob of Serugh and His Times* (Gorgias Press, 2010).

J. Kollamparampil, "Divine Pedagogy on the Road of Salvation and Early Syriac Perspectives," *PdO* 36 (2011): 85–98.

___ *Jacob of Serugh, Select Festal Homilies* (Bangalore: Dharmaram Publications, 1997).

___ *Salvation in Christ According to Jacob of Serug* (Bangalore: Dharmaram Publications, 2001).

J. Konat, "Christological Insights in Jacob of Seruh's Typology as Reflected in his *memre*," *ETL* 77 (2002): 46–72.

___ "A Metrical Homily of Jacob of Serugh on the Mysteries, Types, and Figures of Christ: Authentic or Compilation," *LM* 118 (2005): 71–86.

___ *The Old Testament Types of Christ as Reflected in the Select Metrical Homilies (memrē) of Jacob of Serugh* (Diss. Louvain, 1999).

T. Koonammakkal, *The Church in the Churches: A Syriac Ecclesiology* (Kuravilangad/Sleeva, 2118).

___ *The Theology of Divine Names in the Genuine Works of Ephrem*, Mōrān 'Eth'ō 40 (Kottayam: SEERI, 2015).

C. Lange, "The Mystery of the Son Did Not Journey Without the Church: A Study on Jacob of Serugh's Memra on the Vision of Jacob at Bethel," *Harp* XX (2006): 209–220.

E.G. Mathews and J.P. Amar (tr.), *St. Ephrem the Syrian. Selected Prose Works* (Catholic University Press, 1994).

C. McCarthy (tr.), *Saint Ephrem's Commentary on Tatian's Diatessaron* (Oxford University Press, 1993).

K .McVey (tr.), *Ephrem the Syrian, Hymns* (New York: Paulist Press, 1989).

R. Murray, *Symbols of Church and Kingdom* (Cambridge University Press, 1975); rev. ed. (Piscataway, NJ: Gorgias Press, 2004).

___ "The Lance Which Reopened Paradise: A Mysterious Reading in the Early Syriac Fathers," *OCP* 39 (1973): 224–34.

___ "The Theory of Symbolism in St. Ephrem's Theology," *PdO* 6–7 (1975–76): 1–20.

G. Olinder, *Iacobi Sarugenseis Epistulae quotquot supersunt*, *CSCO* II.45; *SS* 57; 1937.

E. Riad, *Studies in the Syriac Preface* (Stockholm: Almquist & Wiksell, 1988).

F. Rilliet, *Jacques de Saroug. Six Homélies Festales en Prose*, PO 196 (Brepols, 1986).

___ "La Louange des pierres et le tonnerre (Lk.19:40) chez Jacques de Saroug et dans la patristique syriaque," *RTP* 117 (1985): 293–304.

___ "La métaphore du chemin dans la sotériologie de Jacques de Saroug," *StPatr* 25 (1993), 324–31.

G. Scholem, *Major Trends in Jewish Mysticism* (New York: Schocken Books, 1941).

F. Siroli, "Jacob of Serugh and the Lord's Prayer," *Harp* (*forthcoming*, 2020).

C. Stewart, '*Working the earth of the heart*'. *The Messalian Controversy in History, Texts, and Language to AD 431* (Oxford, 1991).

W. Strothmann, *Jakob von Sarug: Drei Gedichte über den Apostel Thomas in Indien* (Wiesbaden, 1976).

E.E. Urbach, *The Sages: Their Concepts and Their Beliefs*, I. Abrahams (tr.) (Jerusalem: Hebrew University, 1979).

R.A. Darling Young, "The 'Church from the Nations' in the Exegesis of Ephrem," *OCA* 229 (1987): 111–121.

INDEX

BIBLICAL REFERENCES

Genesis
  28:14   74: 152
  28:16,17 74: 198, 251
  28:19   74: 223
  28:20   74: 278
  28:22   74: 331
  29   75: 48
  29:1ff   75: 53
  29:9   75: 63
  29:10   75: 64
  29:11   75: 78
  29:15   75: 128
  29:17   75: 254, 304
  29:19   75: 304
  29:18   75: 129
  29:25   75: 203, 208
  29:26–27 75: 218
  29:31   75: 312

Exodus
  32:1–9   75: 255
  32:8,9   75: 255
  34: 33–35 75: 247

Matthew
  6:11   74: 307
  6:34   74: 298, 327
  13:15   75: 312

Luke
  11:3   74: 307
  23:39   74: 115

Ephesians
  2:14   74: 97, 115

Philippians
  2:7   75: 46

1 Corinthians
  7:14   75: 28

INDEX OF KEY TERMS

betrothed (*makrâ*) 75: 44, 86, 90, 107, 169, 182, 236, 245, 277, 281, 307.
bride (*kalthâ*) 75: 85, 185, 193, 203, 244; 74: 245.
bridal chamber 74: 247.
bridegroom (*ḥatnâ*) 75: 70, 92, 169, 185, 194, 203, 285.
Church 74: 30, 50, 201, 222, 230, 235, 239, 243, 289; 75:

5, 38, 69, 86, 94, 98, 105, 111, 136, 144, 238, 243, 251, 258, 263, 275, 281–89, 299, 323, 329.
Church of the Nations 74: 45; 75: 5, 30, 98.
covenant (*qyâmâ*) 75: 126, 155, 164, 212.
Cross, Crucifixion (*ṣlibâ, zqipâ*) 74: 36, 43, 62, 89, 93–120, 158, 167– 177, 225, 299; 75: 139, 142, 296.
depict, portray (*ṣûr*) 74: 26,148, 273, 282; 75:11, 225.
hidden mysteries (*râzê kâsyê*) 74: 126; 75: 184.
hope (*sabrâ*) 74: 160.
image (*ṣalmâ*) 74: 55, 62, 228; 75: 33.
ladder (*sebelṭâ*) 74: 63, 67, 83–89, 95, 131, 166–177, 259, 264.
likeness (*demûtâ*) 74: 12; 75: 22, 294,
love (*ḥûbâ*) 74: 2–6,76; 75: 158.
mysteries (*râzê*) 74: 11–21, 26, 30, 33, 47, 51, 87, 145, 159, 164–165, 202, 219, 224, 240, 242, 247, 274, 289, 311, 324, 333; 75: 1, 36, 50–52, 60, 69, 74, 84, 86, 113, 123, 223, 230, 235, 305, 327, 330.
Moses 75: 247, 250, 259, 271.
Nation 74: 156, 175; 75: 237, 240, 246, 265, 267, 283, 326.
Nations 74: 140, 151–55, 160, 163, 168; 75: 5, 71, 98, 103, 108, 111, 237, 239, 241, 245, 261, 268, 308, 326.

Passion (*ḥaššâ*) 75: 89, 98.
path, way, road (*ûrḥâ*) 74: 15–22, 28, 31, 34, 48, 88, 106, 205, 238–240, 282, 293, 297–299, 304; 75: 1, 7, 19, 41–42, 91, 100, 225, 306.
place (*atrâ*) 74: 21–23, 58, 165, 202, 205, 223, 250 - 255.
providence (*mdabbrânûṭâ*) 75: 228.
repentance (*tyâbûtâ*) 75: 242.
revelation (*gelyânâ*) 74: 13, 74, 79, 81, 119, 127, 158, 180, 193, 199, 215, 229, 249, 271, 301, 306; 75: 50, 264.
secret (mystery, *râzâ*) 75:180, 223, 230, 235.
staff (*ḥuṭrâ*) 74: 35–40, 49, 61.
stone (*kêphâ*) 74: 29, 49, 203, 212, 221–224, 243, 250, 273; 75: 55– 66, 73, 106, 114 - 120.
suffering (*ḥaššâ*) 75: 28, 78–96, 137, 139, 146, 154.
symbol (*râzâ*) 74: 26, 234.
Synagogue 75: 246, 283, 291, 298, 308–20.
tears (*dem'ê*) 75:79, 89–96.
trace (*ršâm*) 74: 276.
types (*ṭûpsê*) 74: 32, 66, 158, 204, 227, 232; 75: 135, 226.
vision (*ḥäzâṭâ, ḥêzwâ*) 74: 66, 73, 79, 82, 119, 122, 130, 179, 202, 217, 233, 311.
Watchers (*'irê*) 74: 56, 100, 196, 258.
wonder (*tehrâ*) 74: 54, 64, 73, 102, 196.

www.ingramcontent.com/pod-product-compliance
Lightning Source LLC
Chambersburg PA
CBHW070303230426
43664CB00014B/2626